A GENUINE LIFE

THE AUTOBIOGRAPHY OF DALE RAGEL

By Dale Edwin Ragel, Sr.

R. L. Craig Publishing

Marietta, Georgia

R. L. Craig Publishing, Marietta, Georgia

 Published 2012.

Printed in the United States of America

Cover photo: A 1930's photograph taken of Russell Ragel, behind the mules and his son Dale Ragel, walking behind the harvester as they cut wheat. Courtesy of Ann Ragel. Enhanced by Darla Huffman.

17 16 15 14 13 12 1 2 3 4 5 6 7 8 9 10

ISBN: 1480204250

ISBN-13: 978-1480204256

TABLE OF CONTENTS

INTRODUCTION

This book is a collection of stories my Dad, Dale Ragel, wrote in his eighties about his own life experiences. They cover from the time he was a small child living on the family farm in central Illinois, recalling his "Rodeo Day" through adulthood, serving in the Army Air Force in England and North Africa during WWII. Later returning to Europe and experiencing life in Spain, France, and England in the nineteen sixties. Some of these stories will make you laugh out loud; others will surely make you cry. In Dad's simple approach to writing, he expresses what he really felt at the time and what was important to him.

As Ann, Shirley, and I work to gather his writings and pictures for this book, Dad is in the last stages of dementia. Over the years, Ann has lovingly typed and organized his work. As we are sorting through the pictures, I glance up at Dad lying peacefully in the hospital bed next to their large dining room window. He has forgotten he wrote the stories and does not even remember the stories themselves. His desire was to share the life he lived, that others might remember the memorable.

Introduction

Thank you, Dad. You have left your family and friends a treasure.

And thank you Ric, Darla, Dianne, and Juandalee for your interest and helping us put his work into print.

Donna Arispe

LEAVING OUR FARM NEAR CAMARGO

December 21, 1922, was a sad day for the Russ Ragel family. My Mother Myrtle was not with us. She had died with the flu on February 27, 1922, so this was a very sad day for all of us indeed. My Dad retarded the spark, turned on the key on our 1914 Model T Ford and stepped on the starter.

Now most people today who are car buffs would say, "A starter on a 1914 Model T Ford? I don't think so." But my Dad had bought the car from the Ford dealer in Farina and it was a demonstrator that they had installed a starter on there.

You could hear the four coils just under the dash of the car start sizzling just like frying bacon, and the old Ford came to life.

We all got in the car to leave our home there near Camargo, Illinois. My three brothers, Herbert the oldest, Virgil and Eugene sat in the back seat, and I being the youngest sat on my sister Nola's lap in the front seat. I could see the tears rolling down her check and feel her sobbing. My Dad was wiping his eyes because we were leaving the farm that was supposed to be a

Dale's birth home. The home was later sold to Ralf and Terry Sapp in 1976. This photo was taken in the summer of 1979.

great financial success.

I took my last look out the side of the car to the barn that sat slightly off to our left. One of the horses had his head out of the top door on the far side of the barn as if he was saying goodbye to us. There was also a well, which we used to get a nice cool drink of water in the summer time. The well was between the barn and the house, but closest to the house, next to the kitchen. This was our last look at the farm.

We drove about 75 miles south of Camargo to our farm just a quarter mile east of St. James, Illinois. St. James is a small town with dirt roads, about 15 houses, a school house, a post office, a Free Methodist Church, a general store, a train station, and a mill for grinding wheat and corn for flour. This is the area where the Ragel and Stine families had settled when they came from Germany in 1834. Nola, Virgil, and I went to stay with Grandpa & Grandma Stine in St. James. Eugene, my brother just older than me, went to stay with Uncle George Ragel, who lived about two miles west of St. James. Herbert went to stay with Uncle Wilbur Ragel who lived about two and a half miles west of St. James. My sister Vida had already left to stay with our uncle, Elmer Stine, my Mother's brother, and his family. At the time, I did not know what had happened to my Dad, but I learned later that he had gone to California by train. In 1922, California seemed like the other side of the world.

OUR FIRST MEAL WITH MY STEPMOTHER

April 12, 1923, I was two years old and it was a very happy time. My dad, stepmother (Edna), and all of us children, except Vida, were back home. We were living in the house my father had built in September 11, 1917, on our farm just a quarter mile east of St. James. This date is inscribed in the foundation on the east side near the south end of the house.

Us children all slept upstairs. Nola was in the last bedroom and us boys in the north bedroom. We all came down for breakfast that first morning to find that my stepmother (we all called her Mother) had breakfast ready. This was a time for all of us to get acquainted. This was the first time we had met our stepmother. She was very loving to all of us children and we were all happy to be together again as a family.

She had prepared a dish she called Float. It was a milk and egg thin pudding sweetened with sugar and vanilla extract. It tasted just scrumptious, served warm with dollops of whipped cream floating around in it. I guess that is why she called it Float. And it was very good.

My oldest sister Nola, who was now 15 years old, had been like a Mother to me since I could remember. However, it took no time until my Mother, by her loving ways, had me coming to her with my skinned knees and stubbed toes.

MY THIRD BIRTHDAY WITH MY STEPMOTHER

That day was a very special day. I was very happy because it was my birthday. My Mother was very happy also, because I was three years old and supposed to be out of that terrible two's stage of my life.

However, I was not really acting like it. Mother had baked me a birthday cake, with delicious looking icing on it.

I voiced my approval by saying, "I want a piece of that yummy looking cake."

Mother said, "No, we are going out in the back yard by those green trees and take a picture of you and the cake."

"No!" I said, jumping around like a jackrabbit, "I want a piece of that cake now! I don't want my picture taken! I want a piece of that cake now," still throwing a hissy fit.

But Mother, in her winning ways and a nice soft voice said, "No, the cake would not look good in the picture with a piece cut out of it. And you would enjoy the picture and cake much more if the cake was complete.

Besides after the picture is taken you can have a piece of this delicious cake."

I thought the quickest way to get the cake was to have my picture taken.

Mother took a 30-dozen egg crate out by the tree in the back yard saying, "Now you sit on this end of the egg crate and I will put the cake over here."

Third Birthday. August 1923.

She picked up her camera and moved back to take my picture and said "Give me a nice big smile and the cake will taste better."

That made me think about that piece of scrumptious cake I was about ready to eat, so I turned on my sweetest smile. That piece of cake sure was good. It was worth waiting for. To this day, the thing that I remember most about this was I did not want my picture taken and the fit I had about it.

WITH MOTHER IN SANTA FE

January 12, 1924, was a very brisk and nippy winter morning. I was hurrying down stairs to get by the heating stove in the living room to get warm. Mother had my Sunday best clothes all laid out on a chair by the stove.

Mother came in from the kitchen and said, "Here Dale. I want you to wear these clothes today."

I said, "Why do you want me to wear these clothes? I only wear them on Sunday."

She said, "We are going on a very long train trip and I want you to look like a nice young man."

"Okay," I said as I was putting on my pants and shirt.

Mother buttoned my shirt for me. After breakfast, we put on our winter coats and gloves.

Dad came in from outside and said, "Are you all ready for me to take you down to the train station?"

Mother said yes, that our suitcases were ready and she had our train tickets.

Dad said, "I will put the suitcases in the back seat. It will be warmer if we all sit in the front seat together."

We all snuggled up in the front seat with me sitting in Mother's lap.

She gave me a little hug and said, "You and I are going on a long train ride to Santa Fe, New Mexico."

I had no idea what that meant. She said a long train ride. I thought that meant a three or four hour ride. It was a short bumpy ride to the train station in our 1914 Model T Ford, with the side curtains on to help keep us warm as we prepared to leave St. James. Dad and Mother unloaded the suitcases. Soon we were all inside the train depot. I was glad to be in where it was warm. It was not long until we heard the train coming. They took our luggage outside and the conductor put it in one of the railroad cars. We said goodbye to Dad, climbed into a different car, and we were on our way to New Mexico. It was exciting to hear the train whistle in the brisk morning air, and the clackety clack, clackety clack of the train wheels as we rolled along, headed for New Mexico.

Dale, Edna, and Eugene Ragel. Undated photo.

Being a curious little boy, I was looking out the window at the cows in the fields and the trees that had lost their leaves, looking like scarecrows, in the distance of course. I was asking my Mother all kinds of questions about everything that I saw. It wasn't long until I thought we should be there and kept asking Mother, "Aren't we there yet?"

We probably were not even out of Illinois by then. A couple of days and ten thousand questions later, we finally arrived in Santa Fe, New Mexico. We took a taxi with our luggage to the apartment that Mother had previously rented. I remember the large kitchen had a hard surfaced floor that I could play with my toy car and the top my Mother had brought so I would have something to play with and to keep me occupied. She also read stories to me quite often, especially at bedtime. I think this was mainly to keep me from asking so many questions.

On nice sunny days, we would take walks through the park and other interesting places. We also went to the post office two to three times a week. The post office had massive doors with big copper plates just above the door handles. The words PUSH was engraved on one copper plate and PULL on the other. Mother taught me to spell those two words and every time we went there, I would repeat them.

She also started teaching me the alphabet. She said, "If you learn the alphabet, I will give you a nice pocket coin purse with 26 pennies in it, one for each letter of the alphabet."

I was quite excited about that. In no time, I had learned the alphabet. This three-year-old boy was very excited about his coin purse full of pennies. My Mother also got me a small heavy metal bank that had a slot in the top to put coins in, but it had little bars under the slot, that would close up when you turned it upside down to shake the coins out, so nothing would come out. I was not too happy about that. However, there was a lock and key you could open up a door on the bottom to remove the money. My Mother kept the key so I would not lose it. I still have that bank today.

When the days started getting warmer by the first part of April, we took that train ride back to St. James. I was all excited about seeing my Dad, three brothers and sister again. After lots of hugs and kisses all around, we were a happy family together again.

ME AND EUGENE FARMING

My brother Eugene, who was two years older than I was, decided we would try farming on a bare piece of ground under the elm tree, out near the barn. It was springtime, the time of the year when all the farmers started plowing the ground to raise their corn and soybeans. Eugene and I got my toy Fordson tractor and a teaspoon from the kitchen to use as our plow. We held the teaspoon behind the tractor to plow the ground. The ground was too hard to plow with our crude equipment. We decided to get a corn knife to dig up the ground and make it nice, soft, and easy to plow.

A corn knife is about two feet long with a wood handle riveted to one end and about one foot is sharpened on the leading edge of the opposite end. It has a wooden handle on one end and the blade was sharpened out about 18 inches from the handle and tapered out to a sharp point.

Eugene was digging up the ground with this knife, and I was following along behind him, with my tractor and plow, with my back toward him. We had plowed a short distance, and I being the curious type, turned around to see how he was doing. However, just as I turned around he had the knife up over his shoulder ready to whack it in the ground. As he raised the knife up over his shoulder, the tip of it just barely nicked my eyeball. There was not a scratch on my face anywhere. I began to cry a little so Eugene turned around to see what was wrong. Now, big brother knew that if I was crying he would be in trouble.

He looked at my face and said, "You're okay! Don't cry!"

I said, "Okay, but my eye hurts." So I quite crying and we went on with our farming.

My oldest sister Nola was out on the back step of the house and she said, "Dale what is wrong?"

I said, "Nothing." I did not want to get Eugene into trouble.

She said, "You come here right now and let me see what is wrong."

I told her no, I was okay, there was nothing wrong.

But she said, "No, I want to see if you are hurt."

I went up to the back porch. She looked at my eye and called Mother and they decided I needed to see a doctor. Mother got me in our Model T Ford coupe and took me to Dr. Owens. Dr. Owens was a doctor and a veterinarian that lived on a farm about three miles west of us. It was a dirty bumpy ride on the dirt road, but it was a bright sunny spring day. My eye felt like I might have a speck of dust in it, but I felt good thinking there is nothing wrong with me. I thought the doctor would get the speck out of my eye, we would go home, and Eugene and I could continue with our farming.

However, Dr. Owens had a different opinion. He said I had to go to the hospital in Centralia, Illinois, which was about 50 miles south of us. We drove back over those bumpy dusty roads to our home. I jumped out of the car and was going to go back to farming, but my Mother said that I had to stay in the house and rest. That was the end of my farming for that spring.

The next morning we were back at the train station with our suitcases in hand. I thought we were in for another long, long train ride. In no time, we heard the train coming. It stopped at the station and the train conductor stepped out of the passenger car.

The train conductor yelled, "All aboard for all points south."

He helped us up the steps into the car and we were on our way with the shrill sound of the train whistle and the clackety clack of the wheels as we rolled along. I looked out the window at the lush green fields and the trees all beautiful with new springtime green leaves.

I thought it was great, and I began to ask Mother all kinds of questions like, "What kind of cow is that? Who owns those cows?"

Mother said, "Never mind. Just sit here in my lap and be quiet. We will soon be in Centralia."

I snuggled down in her lap, but I thought that was a likely story. The last time we were on the train it was two long days and nights."

I felt warm and very comfortable with Mother holding me in her lap. I guess I must have fallen asleep, because it was no time until I heard the train screeching to a stop, and the conductor was helping us down the steps and off the train. We took a taxi to the Centralia Central Hospital.

As we entered in those large swinging doors, I asked Mother, "What kind of place is this?"

She told me that it was a hospital, which did not mean much to me. The desk clerk directed us into the doctor's office.

The doctor examined my eye and said, "Well, we will have to remove the eye. It will take the strength from the good eye if we don't."

Mother screamed, "Oh, no you can't do that!"

Nevertheless, the doctor convinced her removing the eye was the only thing they could do. The nurse brought in a gurney and put me on it.

It felt like three iron bars about six inches apart, lengthwise on the gurney that I was lying on. It was very uncomfortable.

My Mother was holding my hand, telling me everything would be all right, as she walked along by my side holding my hand and trying to comfort me. It made me feel good. I just felt like nothing could go wrong. I really loved Mother and felt warm inside. I wanted her to carry me. Then we came to the operating room door and the nurse told Mother she couldn't go inside.

The nurse assured Mother, "Dale will be okay."

As Mother released the grip on my hand, I screamed "No! No! I am not going anywhere without you."

Dale and Eugene Ragel, 1924.

I tried to get off the gurney and cling to Mother. However, the nurse finally got me loose from Mother and back on the gurney. I was still crying, screaming, flailing my arms, and kicking my legs. I did not want to go anywhere without my Mother. The doctor and nurses held me on the gurney and gave me a shot in the arm.

The next thing I remember, Mother was standing by my side, and I had a large bandage over my right eye. I felt oh so good that Mother was right there at my side. I knew that nothing could go wrong now.

FIRST DAY OF SCHOOL

On September 5, 1926, I was just five years old two weeks prior. Now I was six years old. This was my first day in school. I did not feel comfortable there. I didn't know all of these boys and girls there. I didn't know the teacher.

I said, "I am going home. I don't like it here."

My oldest sister Nola was not there, so I was scared and I was going to go home. Nola had taken me to school to visit one day that spring. Just visiting, with Nola there as my security, was great fun and I felt comfortable. I really enjoyed it. I thought going to school would be fun, but when I got there and was actually in school and Nola was not there, it was entirely different.

The teacher caught me before I got to the door. She gave me a little hug, and said, "You will be okay."

She introduced me to the other boys my age, and I did have two older brothers there, but it was not like my sister being there. I decided to stay, and it was not long until I was playing with the other boys my age.

When class started, the teacher came over to me and said, "Look here Dale. Here is a book with pictures in it. And I will help you read about the different animals."

I got interested in the book and soon forgot about going home. As I was walking home that evening, I was thinking more about getting home to be with my Mother and my sister than about school.

When I got home, Nola gave me a big hug. I felt warm inside.

Nola said, "School will not be too bad even if I am not there."

I said, "Okay, but I enjoyed it much more when you were there. I like to be near you, and it is comforting when I can hold your hand."

MOLINE TRACTOR

Dad hollered at us boys, "Dale! Herbert! Come over here and help me connect the disc to the Moline tractor."

I said, "Sure Dad. We will be right there."

Now, my Dad bought this tractor the one year we farmed in Camargo. He then had it shipped by train to our farm at St. James.

Here I need to explain what a Moline tractor is like. They are probably different from any tractor you have ever seen. They were built in Moline, Illinois, just across the Mississippi river from Davenport, Iowa. The Moline tractor has only two wheels. It is over 5 feet tall, about 12 inches wide, with cleats about 10 inches apart on the circumference of both wheels. The left wheel has cemented the full width and circumference of the wheel. The engine is located on the right side of the tractor frame, balanced over the drive axel, next to the right wheel.

The tractor does not have a seat. The seat is on the implements, the plow, or disc. It does have a set of road wheels, with seat and a draw bar on the back that you can attach other implements to, such as a harrow, wagon or drag, etc. From the seat on any of the attachments, you can easily reach the steering wheel, gearshift lever, clutch, brake, gas lever, or choke. Now the steering wheel was a round steel wheel about 18 inches in diameter, that was placed vertically in front of you, with a handle that was pointed straight back toward you.

It took about 15 turns of the steering wheel to turn from straight ahead to a sharp turn in either direction, or about 30 turns to turn from a sharp right turn to a sharp left turn. The steering wheel has a steel rod about 10 feet long, with a tapered cogwheel on the other end of the rod. The outer end of the cogwheel has a slightly smaller diameter than the end toward the steering wheel. This is so the teeth on the cog wheel will match the teeth on the semicircular arc, which is a half circle gear, with teeth on the top side that mates to the gear teeth on the end of the steering wheel rod. This half circle gear is attached to the frame of the tractor, so as you turn the steering wheel, it forces the tractor's front wheels to turn in the direction you are turning the steering wheel.

After we got the disc all attached to the tractor, Dad told Herbert, "You being the oldest of the boys, get up on the seat and pull the gas lever down about a half inch, and pull the choke out about the same, and I will go and crank the engine, to see if we can get it started."

Herbert said, "What do I do when it starts."

"Just adjust the gas or choke when I tell you."

Herbert said, "Okay."

Dad cranked the engine a few times. It started, ran a couple of seconds, and died. It sounded like large firecrackers going off on the Fourth of July. It scared me, and I ran up to the house as fast as I could. I did not want anything to do with that wild machine. Dad continued to crank the engine. After a little bit, it started and kept running. Then there was really a lot of noise. I went into the house away from all of that noise, shut the door, and looked out the window to see what was happening.

Then Dad got on the tractor seat and drove to the south 20 acres, to disc what he had plowed last week with the tractor. After about 30 minutes, the tractor noise quit so I went back outside. Herbert was working in the machine shed.

I asked him, "What happened to the tractor?"

He said, "I don't know. Let's go see what's wrong."

We saw the tractor had gotten into the netting and barbed wire fence at the north end of the field. Dad hollered at us to bring the crow bar and a hammer to help him get this thing out of the fence. We went back to the machine shed, got the crow bar and hammer, and went on our way to the tractor.

I asked Herbert, "How did he get the tractor into the fence like that?"

He replied, "I guess he didn't start turning that steering wheel soon enough."

I said "Yeah. I guess he sure is going to be mad now."

When we got up to the tractor, Dad said, "This crazy thing don't turn very good on this plowed ground. Help me get this broken fence post and all of this barbed wire off of the wheel so I can back this monster up a little and get it out of here."

I said, "Okay, we will do the best we can."

Dad cranked up the tractor. Herbert used the crow bar to hold the barbed wire of the wheel and I pulled on the broken fence post to help. Then Dad backed up enough to get it off the fence and went ahead with his disking. But he kept it out of the fence after that. The next year, he traded the Moline monster in on a new Fordson tractor. I think he had enough of the monster.

OUR TRIP TO CALIFORNIA

The weather was freezing cold, as this was December 27, 1927. The car windows were all covered with a thick layer of frost. We had all said goodbye to my sister Vida, and Uncle Elmer and family. Vida had lived with them ever since my Mother died in 1922. My Dad, Mother, three brothers, and I, got into our new 1927 Chevrolet and started our trip to California.

We drove about two miles to the small town of Lakewood. Just as we crossed the railroad tracks entering town, we heard this horrible swishing sound right behind us.

Dad said, "What in the world was that?"

A freight train shot behind us, only missing our car by a few feet.

As soon as Mother got her nerves settled enough to speak, she said, "That freight train almost hit us! We could have all been killed!" With a sigh of relief, she settled back down in the seat.

I think us boys were too scared to say anything. The frost was still so thick on the side windows we had not seen the train coming.

We drove on down to our farm near St. James, and got the rest of our clothes for our stay in California.

We were all getting in the car when Mother said, "We are going to be gone for four to five months. Maybe we should lock up the house."

So we all got out of the car to look for the door key, as we normally never locked the door. No one knew where the key was, but after a few frantic minutes, we found the door key and the house was locked.

Dad said, "Well, maybe we are finally ready to leave. I sure hope the rest of the trip goes better than it has so far."

We all got into the car and headed for California.

When we were about 60 to 80 miles east of Dallas, Texas, in hill country, we came over the top of the hill and there was a tractor pulling a road grader. They were grading to smooth off the dirt road surface down at the bottom of the hill just ahead of us. Just then, this big Lincoln sedan passed us, going very fast.

Mother screamed out, "Oh my goodness! They are going to hit that road grader!"

She rolled down the window and tried to flag them down, but it was too late. We could see that he was going to plow right into that road grader. We all started to scream and holler at them, but there was nothing any of us could do. The driver hit that road grader head on. His wife went through the windshield. Her face and arms were all cut up and bleeding profusely. We got out of the car and tried to help them but there was not much we could do and no way to call an ambulance or get any help. The man on the road grader, who lived in the area, seemed to take charge of the situation. He said he would take care of them, and get the lady to the doctor.

We finally pulled around the wreckage and were on our way. We stayed in some cabins in Weatherford, Texas that night.

About three nights later, we stayed in some cabins in Flagstaff,

Arizona. It was on the west side of Flagstaff in the hilly mountainous country. Dad pulled up the hill to our cabin and the engine quit just by the side of the cabin.

We all got out of the car and Dad said, "Well, I guess this will be our home for tonight. Now you boys be careful here in these hills and look out for those swings over there."

He and Mother went in to check out the cabin. Us four boys headed right for the swings, where there were already several boys over there playing.

As we were scampering up the hillside to the swings, Herbert being the oldest, said "Dale, now you be careful don't get near those swings you might get hit.

Now this wasn't Dad talking. Do you think this seven-year-old boy would pay any attention to what his brother said? I don't think so! Nevertheless, I said, "Sure Herbert. I'll be very careful."

It was just after sundown when we got there, so by this time it was getting dark. We were all getting on the swings as they became empty. It was great fun. The swings would swing very high. It was just like you were flying through the air.

I soon got tired and as my swing slowed down I said, "Here Eugene you can swing for a while."

As I was walking away from the swings, in the semi darkness, I walked too close to the other swings. I was hit in the head and knocked down. I started screaming and crying. As I was getting up, I thought it was my fault. I can't get any of my brothers in trouble by crying. I quit crying and we all went up to the cabin.

Mother gave us all a big hug and said, "Go get washed up. I have fixed you all a hot bowl of soup and a sandwich."

We all ate our dinner and went off to bed.

The next morning when we got up, Dad said, "Get washed up and put your clothes in the suitcase. Put it in the car and get in. We will eat breakfast down the road."

We all got in the car and Dad tried to start the car. The battery was dead. When the car had stalled going up the hill last night, Dad forgot to turn the key off. In 1927, it took 12 hours to charge a battery. So we all got out of the car.

Dad said, "Well, I guess we aren't going anywhere today. Why don't you boys go up behind the cabin and play in the woods. I will get someone to charge the battery."

We all scampered up the hill to play in the woods.

As we were climbing up the hill, Virgil exclaimed, "What is that up the hill on the other side of the road? Is that a cave or something?"

We looked up there, and altogether agreed that it would be great fun to go and explore the cave. Away we went, running up to the cave. When we got there, it was more than a cave. We thought that it must be some kind of mine.

"Hey! This is great! Let's see what this is all about," we shouted to one another as we were running down into the mine.

There was no one and no signs that said we could not. The mine was very poorly lit with a very dim light bulb every 100 feet or so. This was a new world for us farmers from Illinois. We had never seen anything like this.

We were asking each other all kinds of questions, "What are these steel tracks for?" and "How do they dig through this solid rock?"

We were all very excited and thought that exploring the mine was great, even if we were a little scared here in the semi darkness and everything very strange to us.

As we were slowly walking along, staying close together, we began to hear this scraping noise.

"What is that," Eugene whispered, as we all huddled up together being very quiet.

Then we heard some men talking off in the distance.

I said, "Let's go see what they are doing."

We passed a slight curve in the mineshaft up ahead and we could see some men shoveling something into these steel-wheeled carts that run on those steel tracks we had seen all the way down here.

One of the workers hollered at us, "What are you doing down here?"

"We are exploring this cave or whatever it is," we said.

"Well, come on down here, and I will tell you all about copper mining. But do your parents know where you are at?"

Herbert, being the oldest, said, "Yes. Dad couldn't get the car started. The battery was dead, so he told us to go play in the woods. But we saw this cave and thought it would be much more fun to explore the cave."

"Well," he said, "My name is Harry and this is not a cave, it is a copper mine."

We all told him our names and he said, "Okay. If you will all sit here on this bench I will tell you all about copper mines, and you can tell your teacher in school that you learned all about copper mines today."

Then Virgil said, "We don't go to school. We are on our way to California. But the car had a dead battery and Dad had to get it fixed before we could continue on the trip."

He said, "You can't get to California by car there are too many mountains and rivers to cross."

I said, "I don't know, but Dad and Mother said we were going to

California."

He said, "I don't think you can make it in a car, but for now I will explain to you all about copper mining."

He proceeded to give us the three-dollar tour, which did not cost us anything. He told us how they drilled holes back into the rock and set off dynamite to break up the rocks, and how they used pick axes to dig out the large rocks etc. I may not remember everything he told us about copper mines but, the day we spent in Flagstaff, Arizona, because the car battery was dead, was the most enjoyable day we had on this entire trip.

When we all got back to the cabin, Dad said, "Where have you been all day? We were worried about you."

"Oh, we went up in the woods like you said and we saw this cave across the road. We went over to investigate, but it was a copper mine. We went about a half a mile or more down into the mine. The men there were loading copper ore into mine carts, and Harry, one of the men, told us all about copper mines and it was very interesting."

Dad said, "Well okay, but you are lucky you didn't get hurt or killed down in that mine. Go in and wash up, Mother is fixing us a nice hot supper, you must all be starved by now."

We had a good hot meal and a good night's rest.

The next morning as we were getting in the car, Dad said, "Well I sure hope this thing starts. I am ready to head for California."

We went through some mighty winding and twisty roads through the mountains, and eventually were out on dirt roads in the rolling hills that were reasonably straight.

We hit a terrible bump in the road and it really shook us all up. My Mother being rather tall hit her head hard on the wood bows in the roof of the car. Mother really cried out and rubbing her head, said, "That really hurt.

And my neck hurts too."

She told Dad, "You need to drive more carefully and watch where you are going."

He said, "We are only going 30 miles an hour, and I couldn't see that ditch across the road until we were right on top of it. Anyway, I don't think your head is hurt that bad."

Mother said, "How would you feel if you hit your head hard enough to break the bow in the roof of the car?"

"Oh, I don't think you broke the bow. You didn't hit it that hard."

I didn't think the argument was really settled yet, because the next time we stopped for gas, we all got out to use the rest room and Dad went around to the passenger side of the car to check the bows in the roof.

He said, "You're right. That bow is really broken."

Mother said, "That is what I tried to tell you, but you knew different. How would you feel if you broke a roof bow with you head?"

There was no answer.

As we headed west toward California, whenever we came to a wash or creek, they had to dig out the banks at a 45-degree angle on both sides using a team of horses and a slip scraper so we could drive through the wash, which was usually dry. Now, the roads were all dirt, or calechi gravel. There was no such a thing as asphalt or cement highways anywhere on this trip. We always carried water to drink, and for the car, extra gas and oil. On the roads crossing Arizona you just follow the tracks of other cars. Sometimes the tracks go on both sides of the cactus; you just follow whichever side you want to. You may only see three or four cars a day, and occasionally, a team of donkeys pulling a wagon. When there is a fork in the road, there might be a wooden arrow pointing in the direction of the next town. We eventually came to Parker, Arizona, crossed the Colorado River Bridge there, and headed for Rice, California.

Mother asked us boys, "Do you know that we are in California now?"

We all answered that it sure looked like Arizona to us. Mother assured us it would look a lot different when we got to Santa Monica, which is where her sister Mary and husband Jim Crossman live. We still had some surprises before we got to Santa Monica. By now, we were used to driving on dirt roads, rocky roads through the mountains, and calechi roads through part of Arizona. Now we were getting into some very sandy roads. In fact, the sand got so deep and fine that they had to build wooden roads over the sand. They were only one lane wide and every mile or two they had a platform about 20 feet long, like a turn out, so if you met someone, one of the cars could pull over on the turnout and the other car would continue on. Traffic was practically nonexistent.

The next day we finally made it to Santa Monica. Uncle Jim and Aunt Mary lived at 938 2nd Street, just the second street up from the Pacific Ocean and just north of Wilshire Boulevard. Just before we turned down 2nd Street, we could see blue water up ahead of us.

I asked Mother, "Is that the Pacific Ocean that you told us about?"

She said, "Yes. That is the largest ocean in the world. Maybe if you are good we can all go down and go swimming one day."

We were all excited and said, "Swimming in the Pacific Ocean! I never dreamed I would ever see the Pacific Ocean let alone swim in it."

Us boys were all asking if she was sure this is where they live.

"Yes," Mother and Dad both chimed in, "We were both there when we were in California in 1923."

Us boys were all jumping around in the back seat, hollering, "We finally made it to see Aunt Mary."

As we drove up, Aunt Mary came running out to the road to see us, hollering "Hello! Hello! I am so glad to see the Ragel." She hugged Mother, all of us boys, and Dad. She said, "Come on in, make yourself at home, and meet Uncle Jim."

We met Uncle Jim. He was more reserved than Aunt Mary was, but greeted all of us as we were introduced to him. Then he went over to the corner of the living room where he had his desk and radio equipment. Us boys were a little shy at first, but Aunt Mary and Mother were talking to us in a nice, soothing, motherly voice.

Aunt Mary said, "Tomorrow we will all walk down to the ocean, and watch those big waves come roaring into the shore. You will like that!"

We had all kinds of questions like, "How far is it to the ocean? Can we go swimming? Can't we go down right now?"

"No. It is too cold, but we will all go tomorrow and have a great time then."

We all said "Okay. We are all so glad we made it to California, and to meet you and Uncle Jim."

LIFE IN VENICE, CALIFORNIA

Dad rented a furnished house at 1472 Washington Boulevard in Venice, California. There were only three houses on the block. On the south side of the street, there was one house toward the east end of the block about one fourth of a mile from us. The other house was next door to us.

We got moved in, brought in our clothes and suitcases, and checked out the house.

Dad said, "Come in here. I need to talk to you boys. I want you to stay out of that street out there. You can play between the street and the alley."

Eugene said, "What is an alley?

Dad said, "Those tracks out there, at the other end of our garage is the alley."

So now, we knew where we could play, between the street and the alley, and it was about one fourth of a mile over to the other house.

About two days later, after breakfast, Mother said, "I am going to walk you to school this morning. Your school is just a short distance across Washington Boulevard and just a little way up 5th Street. I want you to be especially careful crossing the street, and watch to see if any cars are coming. You have to look both to your left and to your right."

We all assured her that we would. We walked on to school, and Mother took us to our classrooms. She said, "Goodbye. And I want you to be especially careful crossing the street, as you know there are a lot more cars on the street here than back home."

We all said, "Goodbye Mom, we will all be careful."

That evening when we got home, we asked Mother if we could walk down to the ocean.

She said, "Yes, but don't go into the ocean, because those waves are very treacherous. When your Dad or I go down with you then you can go out into the water."

We all jumped with joy and said that we would be good and wouldn't go in the water. We headed down Washington Boulevard and when we got down to the ocean, to our great surprise was the largest and tallest roller coaster we had ever seen! We weren't interested in the ocean anymore. We were interested in the roller coaster. We didn't have any money to ride on it but for now, it was fun just to watch it and listen to the clackety clack of all of those steel wheels on the steel track and to see that thing rush downhill and shoot up the other side and around the corner. To start with, it was fun just to watch.

Then Virgil, who proved to be the biggest daredevil of the bunch, said, "I bet that thing would be great fun to ride."

Me, being the youngest said, "I am not sure about that. Don't you hear all of those people on there screaming and hollering?"

"Yeah," he answered, "but I still think it would be a blast."

Someone told us this place was called the Venice Pier, and they have all kinds of rides and things you can spend your money on.

We said, "Great! We will go look at everything."

And we did. On our walk back to the house, we were all excited, telling each other what a great place that was. When we got home, we were all trying to tell Mother at once, what we saw.

Finally, Mother said, "Why don't you all be quiet and let Virgil tell me what this is all about?"

So he said, "This was the greatest place I ever saw. They have a roller coaster there that we can ride in that goes way up in the sky and comes shooting back down. It is on steel tracks and it makes a lot of noise, but it would sure be fun to ride on it."

We were all jumping around and hollering, "Can we have some money to go down and ride on it tomorrow after school, huh can we?" We repeated several times.

Mother said, "Just calm down. When Dad gets home, I will ask him, but I don't think you can go tomorrow evening."

That evening at the supper table, Mother told Dad about the Venice Pier and the roller coaster. She explained that the boys wanted some money to ride the roller coaster. Dad just sat there and kept eating. Then after a minute or so he asked, "How much does it cost to ride the roller coaster?

After a short silence Eugene said, "Dad, it only costs 10 cents to ride the roller coaster. And we can get an ice cream cone for a nickel."

After another short silence Dad replied, "You can all have enough money for a roller coaster ride and an ice cream cone, but not until Saturday. I get paid Friday. Then I will give you the money for your big day Saturday."

We probably did not learn very much at school that Friday, because all we thought about was that roller coaster ride on Saturday.

After breakfast on Saturday, we could hardly wait until Mother said, "It is okay. You can go now, but be careful crossing the streets and while you are at the pier."

After we got to the pier, we watched the roller coaster awhile, then Herbert said, "Well, let's all get on this thing and try it out."

After hearing all of those people screaming and hollering I wasn't sure if I wanted to go on or not. I had never seen anything like this before. I said, "If you are all going, I am going too."

We all screamed and hollered just like everyone else. And we all agreed that it was a real thrill, and great fun. We went back to Venice Pier about once or twice a week all the time that we lived there. Sometimes we just went to watch and listen to the roller coaster. Sometimes, when we had some money, we went to ride on it.

We also went out to visit Aunt Clara quite often. She was a schoolteacher and lived in Rosemead, California. She had Newfoundland dogs that were trained to pull a little wagon. The dogs would pull us back and forth on the sidewalk in front of her house, which was great fun because we didn't have to push the wagons. We let the dogs do all the work. We visited Aunt Clara several times while we lived in Venice. She always had some goodies for us to eat and she wanted us to exercise her doge by letting them pull us in the wagons, which we enjoyed very much.

I remember one time we had a very heavy rain, and Washington Boulevard was flooded. The water was about 8 to 10 inches deep. There was an older man standing out in the middle of the street, with cars going by him in both directions, standing in the deep water with boots, rain coat and rain hat on. He was giving every car that came by a Heil Hitler salute, and kicking his right leg out in front of him with the salute. We stood out in front of our house watching him, and getting a big laugh about it. Mother had gone over to her sister Mary's house, and Dad was not home from work yet. So we were standing in our yard mocking the guy in the street. We were laughing at him and laughing at each other. We had nothing else constructive to do. When the parents are not at home, you have to do something that you are not supposed to do.

One Sunday in the first part of April, right after breakfast, Dad asked us if we would like to take a ride out to San Bernardino, and look at the orange groves and the beautiful countryside.

"Sure, that sounds like great fun," we all replied, "When can we go?"

"As soon as you get ready and loaded in the car, we will be on our journey."

We all jumped in the back seat with Mother and Dad up front and shouted, "Ok, let's go." And we were off to see the green countryside and orange groves.

We had been driving over an hour and I asked the same old question, "Aren't we about there yet?"

Dad said, "Any minute now. Don't you see all of those beautiful green orange trees, just loaded with those golden yellow, sweet oranges?"

"Oh yes," I said, "Can we stop and get some of those oranges to eat?"

"Yes, we will find a place very soon where we can buy some oranges."

It wasn't long until we saw a large building with several truckloads of bright golden colored oranges. We stopped and all got out of the car and watched them unload the oranges onto a wide conveyor belt. As the belt moved along there were some men and women standing on one side of the belt taking off the oversized and over ripe oranges.

Dad asked one of the men, "What do you do with the oranges you take off the belt?"

He replied, "We sell them right over there by that building. These others are boxed and shipped back east."

We walked over to the building and there was a man there selling the oranges. Dad asked him, "Are these oranges any good?"

"You bet!" he said slicing one of them in about six slices. "Would you like to try one?"

"Sure," we said in unison.

The man gave us each a slice, and they sure were good and full of the nice sweet orange juice.

Dad asked, 'How much are the oranges?"

"Twenty five cents for one of those 40 pound burlap bags full," he said.

Dad gave him a quarter and loaded the bag of oranges into the car. We all got in the car and headed back to Venice.

After we got out on the road Dad said, "Why don't you give me one of those oranges, 'cause they sure were good."

We opened the bag and gave Mother and Dad an orange and one for all of us boys. As we peeled and ate the oranges, saying how delicious they were, we all thought they were the best oranges we had ever eaten.

Then Mother gave us a towel and said, "Wipe your hands and face, and put all of the orange peelings in the towel and give it back to me."

We did and settled down to look out the window at all of the large fields of beautiful green trees, and the branches almost breaking with those luscious golden colored oranges on them. It was not too long until us boys fell asleep in the back seat of the car after enjoying a day in the country.

FROM SANTA MONICA TO ST. JAMES

It was Sunday afternoon. We were all over at Aunt Mary's house in Santa Monica saying our good-byes. Mother came over to me and gave me a long tender hug.

"I won't be going back to St James with you."

"You won't be going home with us?" I exclaimed with tears in my eyes. I sobbed, "Mother, I need you. I want you to go home with us."

Giving me another little hug, she said, "I am coming back on the train and I will be there as soon as the weather gets warmer. You know how I always get sick with the cold damp weather here in Illinois."

"I know," I sobbed, "but I will sure miss you."

About that time, Dad said, "I guess we better get home to get our clothes and things loaded in the car so we can leave real early tomorrow morning."

We all started getting into the car. I was still standing there sobbing. Mother picked me up and as she was carrying me over to the car, she whispered in my ear, "I love you."

I sobbed out, "Mom, I love you, too," as she sat me down in the back seat of the car. As Dad pulled away from the curb, we were all waving goodbye to Mother and Aunt Mary, standing on the front lawn waving to us.

On our way back to our house in Venice, I was thinking of the time that Mother and I spent in Santa Fe and the time she took me to the hospital in Centralia and stayed there with me. I sure had many pleasant and fond memories of my mother and I did not want to go home without her. I also thought maybe the reason she did not want to go home with us was because of the lump she got on her head when Dad hit that chuckhole and she broke the wooden bow in the top of the car on our way out to California. She did not want any more of that.

After we got home and got the car loaded, Dad said, "You all better get to bed because we are leaving early in the morning. And you all need a good night's sleep."

When Dad said early, he meant early. About one o'clock Monday morning, he came into our bedroom and shouted, "Okay, boys it is time to get up and get out of here. Be sure we haven't left any of our belongings here."

In no time we were up, made a quick trip through the house, and out to the car.

Dad said, "Which ever one of you is wide awake can sit up front with me to help keep us on the right road."

Virgil took the job. The rest of us got in the back seat and we were off down Washington Boulevard.

As we were leaving Venice, I was thinking of my mother and wishing she would be in the car with us and that I was sure going to miss her. But on down the road a ways my mind started wondering. I was thinking of all the good times we had down at the Venice Pier, on the roller coaster, rushing down that first hill with the wind in our faces, screaming our lungs out, and enjoying every minute of it. If we did not have money to ride on it, it was great fun to watch and listen to the screaming and the clackety clack of the steel wheels on the track as the roller coaster shot by us on that downhill run. I guess I will never forget the winter of 1928 that we spent in Venice, California. Since it was the middle of the night, I guess it was not long until us boys in the back seat fell asleep.

It was starting to get daylight, and we had stopped at the agriculture inspection station, just before you cross the Colorado River into Parker, Arizona. The fruit inspection station had a stop sign by this small building. The building was about 8 feet by 12 feet, with a door facing the road.

As Dad was getting out of the car he said, "I guess I will go knock on the door to see if anyone is home."

A minute or so after he knocked, the fruit inspector came and opened the door part way. He was in his pajamas, but he asked, "Do you have any citrus fruit in the car?"

"No," Dad answered him.

At that, the inspector shut the door and we were on our way. We had not driven very far into Arizona until we had a flat tire. Dad pulled over to the side of the road.

"Everybody out! Pull the back seat forward and get the jack, tire pump, tire iron, lug nut wrench, and the can of inner tube patching stuff out."

Herbert and Virgil, being the oldest, set about getting all of that stuff out from behind the seat.

As they handed it out to Dad, he said, "Herbert, you put this jack under the axel of the left rear wheel, and after I loosen the lug nuts, you jack up the car."

Eugene and I watched that for a little while, and then Eugene said, "Dale let's go out behind the car and see if we can hit that cactus out there with some of these rocks."

We enjoyed ourselves with rock throwing until they got the flat fixed, and we were ready to go again.

"Okay," Dad said, "load those tools in behind the seat, and we will be on our way."

It seemed like every few hours we were stopped again fixing flat tires that day. As we pulled in beside the cabins where we were going to stay that night, Dad looked down at the speedometer.

"Well, we had five flat tires today, but we still drove 500 miles. I sure feel like it too. This has been a long day. I think we have been on the road for 18 to 20 hours today, and I am ready for a good night's sleep."

We had several more flat tires, and we used up all of the two-gallon cans of oil that dad bought before we started. They sure don't make cars and tires like they used to. Aren't we lucky!

We stopped in St. Elmo, Illinois, on our way home. This is about six miles north of St. James, our hometown. Nola had rented a room and was going to High School there. The weather was cold, damp, and raining. This is the reason mother did not want to come back until the weather was warm, nice and sunny and cheerful. As we got closer to St. Elmo, I began to get antsy and excited. I knew it wouldn't be long until I got to see my sister Nola. She was like a mother to me, especially after my mother died and before my stepmother became part of the family.

When we stopped at Nola's apartment, I was the first one at the door. I could not wait to give Nola a big hug and kiss and she was sure glad to see all of us. I could not get a word in edgewise. I wanted to tell her all about the fun we had in California and about all of the things we had seen on our trip.

But Dad thought it was time for us to get on down to the farm, so he said, "Everybody back in the car. Let's finish this trip and see if our house is still there. We have been gone so long."

We all hopped in the car and were on our way. It took about 30 minutes to drive down there on those muddy slick roads.

I kept saying, "Dad don't let this thing slide off in the ditch or we will never get home."

Dad said, "Don't worry, Dale, I have been driving on muddy roads ever since I've had a car."

As we pulled in the driveway, us four boys stood up hollering, "We made it home and the house is still here!"

Dad got out of the car, went up to the side door of the house, and unlocked the door.

I said, "Alright, we didn't have to look for the key. I thought maybe we had left it in California."

It was not long until Dad had a big roaring fire going in the heating stove, and we all stood around the stove enjoying that nice wood fire, and the smell of oak wood burning away.

Dad said, "It is nice to go on vacation but it is nice to be home again."

RIDING OUR WAGONS IN THE HAYMOW

"Why don't we go and sweep the haymow floor, then ride our wagons up there. We could have a figure-eight racetrack. That would be great fun," I said to my brothers, Virgil and Eugene.

Virgil, being the oldest, was more of a dare devil than Eugene and I. It was one of those warm rainy days in May 1928. We could not work in the fields so this seemed like a good day to have some fun riding our wagons.

Virgil said, "Yeah! Eugene, why don't we go and get a couple of brooms to sweep the floor clean. And Dale, you can get a pitch fork and push that little bit of hay up in the corner."

I said, "Sure. I can do that."

We were all really excited about being able to ride our wagons on a hard surface. All we ever rode on was dirt in the barnyard or grass in the front lawn. We got that wood floor all cleaned up and it looked like a great place to race our wagons. The wheels could get good traction and we could go real fast on that clean wood floor. We could hardly wait to get started.

I said, "Virgil, why don't you and Eugene go and get the wagons and hand them up to me."

They ran to get the wagons. Eugene said, "This is going to be great fun riding on that smooth hard wood floor."

They handed the wagons up tongue first, so I could get a hold of the tongue and pull them up into the haymow. We were all getting real excited about racing each other on that smooth wood floor. Virgil and Eugene got in the wagons and rode first. They were screaming and hollering, and trying to see how fast they could go. But we soon found out that Virgil's wagon, with the steel bands on the wheels for tires, had very little traction on the wood floor. It was difficult to turn if you were going very fast. The smaller Radio Flyer red wagon that belonged to Eugene and I had rubber tires. It was much easier to guide and control the wagon when going fast.

I could hardly wait for my turn to ride. I was getting so excited I kept saying, "Eugene! My turn! My turn!"

Eugene let me have my turn. I really liked coasting on that smooth floor. You could go real fast and it was real easy to guide the wagon in the direction you wanted to go. We decided to have a figure-eight race. Since there was about a four-foot-by-four-foot hole on the south side of the haymow, we had to design our figure-eight racetrack around that. The hole was where there was a ladder to climb up, and where we threw the hay down to feed the cows and horses. Then we all took our turns to try it out. It was a lot of fun, but Virgil had trouble getting the wagon to go in the direction he pointed it because of the steel wheels.

After we all had several turns riding the figure-eight track, Virgil said to Eugene, "Why don't we have a race on this thing? I can keep this headed in the right direction now."

I said, "You line up here at this end and I will start you off."

So they lined up even at the west end of the haymow. I was the starter. I stood beside them with my hand up in the air.

"Get ready! GO!"

I dropped my hand and they were off. On the third time around Virgil came off of the east end totally out of control, in the lead, but as he got it headed east, it was headed right for the hole in the floor. He did everything he could to get the wagon to turn to the right in order to miss the hole, but to no avail.

I hollered at him, "Virgil! Get off of that thing NOW!"

If he went down with the wagon, I was afraid he would get badly hurt. I breathed a sigh of relief when I saw he got off the wagon in time. The wagon went down through the hole, without the driver. Virgil wasn't hurt. Maybe a little scared.

He went down and checked out the wagon and said, "It's okay." He handed it back up to me tongue first and we continued riding, and racing once in a while, the rest of the afternoon. However, no more wagons through the hole in the floor.

CULTIVATING CORN

We had just finished breakfast. Dad told Eugene and me, "You two are going to cultivate corn today."

"Dale, I want you to drive the mules and Eugene you will operate the cultivator shovels. The mules are in the barn, all harnessed up, and ready to go. I want you two to go and get the mules out of the barn and hitch them to that cultivator over under the Elm tree."

I said, "Sure, Dad we can do that."

It was the first of July 1929. I was only eight years old, but I felt like a young man. I am going to drive those mules all by myself and we are going to cultivate corn. I was really proud of myself. I almost burst the buttons off my overalls.

After we got the mules hitched to the cultivator, Dad came over and told me to get up there on that board nailed on the back of the cultivator tongue.

"That is where you will sit while you drive the mules. Drive over to the 20 acres of corn just east of the barn. Eugene, you get on the cultivator seat and I will walk over and show you how to get started."

I was just a little bit scared taking the lines and sitting there just behind the mules on top of the cultivator. Nevertheless, I never let on that I might be scared. I felt like a million bucks sitting up there and driving the mules all by myself.

I am going to drive those mules all by myself and we are going to cultivate corn.

Dad said, "Dale, turn in there on that first row and head those mules toward the other end of the field. Keep that cultivator tongue right over the row of corn and Eugene you guide those shovels, so you plow out most of the weeds, but don't plow out any of the corn."

Now the corn was about 18 inches tall, so there was no trouble to see what we were supposed to do but it took a little practice to actually do it. Our dad and older brothers had used the mules cultivating before so it made it easier that the mules knew what they were supposed to do. It was a quarter mile to the other end of the field.

As we neared the far end, I started thinking, "I have to turn these mules around and get on that row right next to us." I was a little apprehensive about that, but when we got to the end of the field, I pulled back on both of the lines and said, "Whoa!" That means stop in mule language. Then I pulled hard on the left line and said, "Haw, darn you! Haw!" Left, in mule language. We got turned around and on the next row of corn. I slapped the mules a little on the rump with the lines and said, "Giddy-up!" Go. And we were on our way back on the second row. We kept this up until just before noon.

It's noon when the sun is straight overhead between east and west. All farmers learn to tell time by the sun. In fact, no one in our family owned a watch. We all told time by the sun. If it was cloudy, you just make your best guess. If you never owned a watch, you got good at telling the approximate time without one.

At approximately noon, I drove back into the barnyard.

I said, "Eugene, if you go and feed the mules there in the barn, I will go and pump water for them."

We unhitched the mules and they automatically went to the watering tank. The mules automatically went to the barn to eat after they were through drinking.

As we went into the house to wash up for our dinner, Mother said, "Well, how did cultivating corn go this morning?"

I said, "Just fine." I felt just like a young man driving those mules all by myself. "It was great fun!"

She said, "Well, you just got here at the right time. Dinner is just ready. I guess you are really hungry. You have been out there farming all morning."

I said, "Yeah, we are ready for dinner." We all sat down and enjoyed a very good dinner because we were hungry.

After dinner, I said to Eugene, "Why don't we get some of those firecrackers, and see if we can blow some cans up in the air."

We went and got some firecrackers and matches and blew up several tin cans.

And then Dad came out and said, "I think it is about time to hitch those mules up to the cultivator and get back out cultivating."

I said okay and we hitched up the mules and went back out to cultivate corn. We cultivated about three rounds and I had just turned the mules around and headed back up through the field when I stopped the mules to rest them for a couple of minutes.

I said to Eugene, "I wonder what old Molly would do if we put one of those little one inch firecrackers under her tail."

Eugene said, "Oh she would probably switch her tail, she would think it was a horse fly biting her."

I got one of the firecrackers and a match out of my two front pockets. I didn't carry matches and firecrackers in the same pocket. I put the firecracker under, and sort of beside, old Molly's tail. Now Eugene is on the seat of the cultivator, and I am on that board just behind the mules and I struck the match and lit the fuse on the firecracker.

When it went off, I guess Molly thought that was the biggest horse fly she ever felt, because she flipped her tail up in the air, passed gas three or four times on a dead run. She was dragging the cultivator, and Toby, the other mule, at about a 30-degree angle across the cornfield. She was plowing out corn and throwing dirt up in the air. I was scared to death, holding on to the board seat with one hand, and pulling back on the lines with the other hand hollering.

"Whoa! Whoa! Whoa!"

However, old Molly is not about to stop. After she got to the far side of the field and half way to the far end I finally got her stropped.

I turned around to Eugene and said, "Well that was a pretty good ride while it lasted, but I sure am glad it's over. I was scared there for a while."

Eugene was laughing like crazy, but said, "I guess we won't try that again. Now what do we do?"

I said, "Well it seems like everything is still all together and Molly has calmed down. I'll drive back to the end of the field and we'll continue cultivating corn."

Which is what we did.

About a day and a half later, we had finished cultivating the 20 acres of corn. Dad came out to look at it.

He said, "It looks like you plowed out a little corn here, what happened?"

I said, "I don't know, old Molly must have been stung by a bumble bee or something. She was awful hard to control there for a while."

Dad said, "Well, we have a lot of corn to cultivate yet. Do you think you and Eugene can do the job?"

I said, "Sure Dad. We have it figured out now." I thought to myself, we had better not use any more firecrackers.

Dad said, "Virgil and I will take our two cultivators and go up and cultivate the corn on the Lovett farm. I want you and Eugene to go over to the Lowery farm and start cultivating corn there tomorrow."

I said, "Okay, Dad. We can do that."

I was glad I was not fired from the job because I was proud of myself. It felt good when I was up there driving those mules all by myself.

But no more firecrackers.

RAISING TURKEYS

It was Tuesday, April 30, 1929, and the one hundred baby turkeys my Mother ordered from the hatchery had just arrived. Mother is so excited because this is her pride and joy.

She said, "Okay, Dale. You and Eugene will have to help me feed, water, and take care of these baby turkeys."

Now, baby turkeys are very fragile and easily pick up diseases from other animals. We had cleaned and disinfected the brooder house, so they would not pick up any germs. The brooder house has a kerosene-fired heater, with a hood that spreads out about eight feet that angles down to keep the heat on the floor to help keep the turkeys warm. The turkeys need to be kept warm so they won't crowd together and be smothered.

Mother said, "Now, Dale. You go and carry the water out to the brooder house and fill their drinking container. And Eugene, you get the sack of turkey feed out of the smoke house and fill the turkey feeders about a quarter full."

Eugene and I were just ten and eight years old respectively, so I am real excited and proud of being a part of this turkey-raising project. We had not raised turkeys, nor seen any raised in this part of the country. So I felt like we were pioneers, doing something new and I had a part in helping raise them.

After we got the feed and water ready for the turkeys and Mother got the heater going, she raised up and said, "As soon as it gets a little warm in here we will bring the baby turkeys out to see if they like their new home."

As we walked into the kitchen, we could hear the baby turkeys in their boxes chirping away, probably saying, "I wonder when we will get to eat."

Mother told Eugene and me each to take one box of turkeys, and she took the other two boxes out to the brooder house.

"Now we will see how these turkeys like their new home," Mother said as we set them out of the boxes.

We had not raised turkeys, nor seen any raised in this part of the country. So I felt like we were pioneers, doing something new and I had a part in helping raise them.

At first they seemed to just stand there trying to figure out where they were. It wasn't long before they were running around chirping at each other, trying to find something to eat.

These little balls of frizz running around here don't realize they could be someone's Thanksgiving dinner this November. As we were walking back toward the house, Mother told Eugene and me that all three of us would go back about every hour to see how they were doing.

"But now I want you two to go out in the garden and hoe and rake the west side of the garden to get the ground ready to plant green beans and peas. You know we have to eat also, just like those turkeys do."

We weren't so excited about hoeing and raking in the garden, but we walked slowly out there.

I said to Eugene, "We do this about every day. It isn't very exciting is it?"

"No, but I guess it is something we have to do anyway," he said.

About three o'clock, Mother came out to the garden and said, "Okay, it is time to go and check on the turkeys. Dale you are responsible to see that the turkeys have clean water all the time, and Eugene it is your responsibility to see that the feeders are full at all times."

As Mother was adjusting the heater to keep the turkeys warm, I thought to myself, "Now this is a big responsibility for me. I will need to be very serious about my work, because I want those turkeys to stay healthy."

We went out to check the turkeys again right after supper, and then as Mother was doing the dishes she said, "We need to check the turkeys again before we go to bed, to be sure they aren't crowding together, and that the heater is adjusted okay for all night."

We continued this routine for about two weeks, before and after school.

Then on Saturday, April 11th as we finished breakfast, Mother asked Dad, "Will you pull the brooder house down to the south end of the cow pasture for me today?"

Dad replied, "Well I am awful busy planting corn today, can't that wait for a few days until I get the corn all planted?"

"No. Those turkeys need to be outside in the sunshine and fresh air away from these hogs and chickens. I want these turkeys to stay healthy, and they are in urgent need of exercise, and fresh air now."

Dad's answer was, "Well, okay if it has to be done, I will go ahead and do it. Dale, will you get that log chain out of the garage, and take it out to the brooder house?"

I got the chain and took it out to the south end of the brooder house. It has two 2 by 8 inch timbers, running the length of the building with holes and a clevis attached. I hooked the log chain to the clevises and then I went inside the brooder house to help Mother.

"Will you take the water containers outside and empty them," she asked, "and I will turn the fire out on the heater. We don't want any accidents while moving this brooder house."

We got out and fastened the door shut, and went around to the other end where Dad was with the mules.

"Well, everything is ready, but be very careful, we don't want to hurt any of the turkeys," Mother said.

We all walked along together and about two hundred feet from the south end of the farm, Mother said, "Right here is a very good place for these turkeys." Mother breathed a sigh of relief and said, "I sure am glad we got the turkeys out here in the clean air and field for them to play, eat bugs, and get some exercise."

Once Mother thought the turkeys looked okay, we had to haul all of the water and feed down there for them.

"And how are we going to do that?" I asked.

"We will use my car. We will get that eight gallon cream can and fill it with water, and take the feed down as we need it," she replied. The car she was referring to was a 1929 Chevrolet coupe.

The brooder house has a small side door, with a ramp so the turkeys or chickens can go in and out, when they want to.

Mother said, "Dale you and Eugene can go back to the house and work in the garden for a while. I am going to stay here and see that the turkeys get out and get some sunshine and exercise, and that they don't get lost."

Eugene and I slowly walked back to the house. We were in no hurry to start working in the garden again. We got the hoe and rake, and went to work.

About noon Mother came out to the garden saying, "You can come in and rest a little while, and we will get a bite to eat."

After dinner, as Mother was washing the dishes she asked Eugene and I to go and fill that eight gallon can with water, get a bag of feed, and put it in the trunk of her car. Both of us struggled to get that water can and bag of feed in the trunk.

About that time Mother came out to the car and said, "You two get in the car and we will go down to see how the turkeys are doing."

We were really happy now getting to ride in Mother's new car, and getting to feed and water the turkeys. This was like playing, as we pulled up to the brooder house.

"First we need to see if the turkeys are okay," Mother said.

Most of them were outside enjoying the nice warm spring day. Mother was feeling good also, as she was doing what she wanted and liked to do. We watched the turkeys playing outside for a while.

After a little bit Mother said, "Dale, you and Eugene go in, feed and water the turkeys, then we will see if we can get all of the turkeys back inside."

As soon as the turkeys were settled down, eating and drinking, we all got into the car and went back to the house.

As we got out of the car Mother told us, "Dale you go and bring the cows up and put them into the barn, and fasten the milk cows into their stanchions. Eugene you can go feed and water the hogs."

When we had that all finished, we thought we were through for the day. No, that was not the case. Mother said, "Now you can take the two buckets and milk the cows. Eugene you better milk old Blackie, because she sometimes tries to kick while milking her."

As we start toward the barn, Mother hollered after us, "Don't forget that after you milk each cow, to bring the milk up here and pour it through the strainer into this ten gallon milk can. Also, you can give the cats some milk in the cats dish there in the barn."

As we were milking the cows, the cats came up begging for milk, when they were about four feet away, we would squirt milk into their mouths. They really liked that, but they knew they would get fed before we went to the house. We had finished milking the seven cows, and taken all the milk up to the screened-in porch

Mother came out and said, "Supper is ready. Your Dad and Virgil just came in from the field. You know your Dad never comes in from the field until it gets dark. So why don't you two get washed up, we will be ready to eat here in a few minutes."

After we had finished supper and Mother was doing the dishes, she exclaimed, "I need to go and check the turkeys before we go to bed."

I asked Mom, "Can I go with you to check the turkeys?"

"Okay," she said, "I will be ready to go in a few minutes."

After we got in the car, I asked Mom, "Will you make me a shirt from one of those FUL-O-PEP feed sacks?" I wanted the FUL-O-PEP letters to be down the front of my shirt where the buttonholes are.

Mom said, "Don't you think that would look funny?"

"No, Mom. I think it would look great. Don't you think I am full of pep?"

She laughed and said, "Yeah. I will see what I can do."

As we walked into the brooder house, Mother said, "I think I will start the heater and turn it on real low heat for the night."

After watching the turkeys for a while to see if they liked the heat or not, we got in the car and drove back to the house. I was feeling good. Mother was going to make me a shirt, and I felt real important getting to help with the turkeys and to ride with Mother in her car. This was about the routine for the summer. Helping Mom with the turkeys, working in the garden, milking the cows, and helping Dad in the fields. Mother did make me the FUL-O-PEP shirt, which I thought was the greatest, and I wore it with pride.

Around the first of October, Mother began talking about selling the turkeys. She said, "The price is real high right now, and I want to sell them in plenty of time, so they can be ready for Thanksgiving."

I was not too happy about that. I asked, "Is that what we raised these turkeys for, so someone can eat them?"

"Well yes. In fact, we are going to have one for Thanksgiving dinner," Mother replied.

I thought to myself, "I never ate turkey before. I do not think I am going to like it."

On October 15, someone came in a big truck with many chicken coops on the back. Mom went out and talked with them and they drove down to the brooder house. I wondered why we hadn't let the turkeys out that morning. But I did not go down to watch them put the turkeys in the coops and load the truck. Instead, I went outside, petted my dog, and played with him. I was not happy with that man taking all of our turkeys.

As he drove away, Mom came over to where I was petting the dog and said, "Dale, I know you are not happy about me selling the turkeys. But I needed the money. I paid off the loan on my car. And your oldest sister, Nola, really wants to go to nursing school. I checked around and found the best hospital for nurses training at Burnham City Hospital in Champaign. So I am going to pay for the full three years."

I gave her a big hug and said, "I love you Mom. I love you very much. And you have been very good to all of us kids."

She gave me another hug and said, "And I love you too."

MY WORLD FELL APART

On April 3, 1931, with my lunch pail in hand, I walked to the one-room schoolhouse out in the country. I walked along without a care in the world, just enjoying the sunshine on a nice warm spring morning. Life could not be better for a 10-year-old boy. Unaware my world would fall apart that day.

Dad pulled up beside me with a team of horses hitched to the wagon. Dad said in a rather stern voice, "Dale, hop up on the wagon, I have something I need to discuss with you."

He didn't seem to be in a very good mood. I thought to myself, what have I done? Now, I must be in trouble about something.

I said, "What is the trouble Dad? Have I done something wrong at home?" Since I had been staying with my Aunt Alice Lowery, I did not know what was going on at home.

Dad said, "No you haven't done anything wrong. It is your Mother. She is leaving us. She is on her way to California, and she wants to take you with her."

I was rather shocked at mom leaving us. In fact, I was speechless at first. I started to cry because mom was always as good to all of us children, especially me, as I was the youngest.

As I was sobbing I said, "Dad, can I go home just to say goodbye to mom?"

Dad said, "No. That would just start another big argument. I would rather leave things just as they are."

"But Dad, she has been so good to me, I need to go and give her a big hug and say goodbye to her."

Dad said, "No, it is better this way. Anyway, you will soon get over it. We are going out to our farm in Effingham County and stack hay. She won't be able to find you there, as there aren't any roads that actually lead back to the farm."

I did not want to go and stack hay, I felt all queasy inside, and I

Russ Ragel Family. Left to right: Virgil, Dale, Nola, Russ, Herbert, Eugene, and Vida. Undated photo.

could not imagine life without Mom. She was actually my stepmother. My mother had died with the flu when I was eighteen months old. She was always there when I needed her. She would bake a cake for my birthday, and she took me to Centralia to the hospital when I got my eye hurt in April 1926. No mother could have been any better to me than she was. I really loved her and knew I would really miss her. I sat there on the board of the frame hay wagon, sobbing as we drove along thinking about Mom all by herself in her 1929 Chevrolet coupe heading for California. I knew it was a very long trip, since we had just gone there in the winter of 1927 and 1928. It was mostly dirt roads all the way to California. In west Texas and Arizona there were not many road signs to give you directions. I could just see my Mother out there all by herself trying to be sure she took the right road. I felt sorry for her too.

About that time, Dad stopped the horses and said, "Dale, will you get off and open the gate so we can drive across the field back to our farm?"

I jumped off and opened the gate but was still thinking about my poor mother out there all by herself on that long, long road on her way to 938 Second Street, Santa Monica, California.

Footnote: Mother even saved up enough money to send my oldest sister, Nola, to nursing school in 1930. This was during the great depression. Mom was determined that Nola would get to nurse training. Mother sent me a Christmas package of dried fruit, dates, figs, and apricots. She also sent birthday cards for many years. I do not know if I ever sent her a thank you letter or not. However, in January of 1946 just after I got my discharge papers from the Air Force I went by to see her on 2nd Street in Santa Monica, California. She had bought a fruit farm in Fontana, California and lived there until just before WWII. She sold her fruit farm to Kaiser Steel Mill and moved back in with her sister, Mary, in Santa Monica. We went to visit her several times before my family and I moved to Seville, Spain in September 1962. My Mother passed away in January 1964.

Through much research, I found out she was buried in the Tuscola cemetery in Tuscola, Illinois.

BARNYARD RODEO

There was a cool drizzle of rain Sunday afternoon March 1932. My three brothers, Herbert, Virgil, Eugene, and I walked out to the old barn trying to think of something to do. Mother had left us and moved to California about a year ago. Dad was not at home. Us four boys were lonesome, bored, and restless. We needed something exciting to do.

"Why don't we get that old ladder and climb up on that big straw stack just east of the red barn and slide down on the animals that are eating at the straw stack and have a rodeo of our own," I suggested.

That changed our mood from doom and gloom to great excitement.

"But Dad told us not to climb on the straw stack anymore," Virgil told us.

I replied, "I know, but we will be up there just a short while, and it will be great fun. He isn't home anyway."

Herbert and Virgil ran off to get the ladder. Now this straw stack is about 180 feet long in a semi-circle and about 18 feet high. The cows and horses had eaten back into it about 6 feet on the inside of the semi-circle, so they were protected from the wind there. Herbert and Virgil came with the ladder and we walked out to the straw stack. I suggested we put the ladder up on the backside of the straw stack from where the animals are eating. That way we wouldn't scare them away. So we all climbed up on the straw stack, and walked over to the other side.

We could see there were several horses, cows, bulls, steers, and mules eating away. After all, we had 36 head of cattle. I asked if anyone was going to ride that big old Holstein bull. I never got an answer. I can understand why. He is a little bit mean sometimes. After we picked out which animal we wanted to ride, we laid down on our stomach, near the edge of the straw stack just above the animal we wanted to ride. We pushed off, hoping for the best, trying to see who could stay on the longest. My first choice was Beauty, the horse. I had ridden her quite a lot, of course with a saddle and bridle, and she was used to me riding her. As I was sliding down toward her back, I was concentrating on getting a good grip on her mane. When I hit her back it scared her, and she was off like a shot and headed toward the barn. Then all of a sudden, she made a quick left turn, headed out to pasture, and dumped me off in the grass. I was excited and proud that I stayed on that long. She was scared and running at full speed.

I got up off the grass, climbed up the ladder to see what I could pick for the next ride. Eugene was up there looking also. I asked him if he was going to try the big Holstein bull.

His answer was, "No, I will leave him for you."

"No," I said, "I don't think so. This time I am going to look for one of the calves or an old cow."

Actually, I lined up with one of the young heifers. My heart was pounding, I was a little bit scared, but you get a very thrilling ride. I lay down on my stomach, on the edge of the straw stack and slid down onto the heifer's back. She let out a big bellow, started bucking and kicking like crazy. I didn't stay on very long. That young heifer was a bucking machine.

We were all having a blast watching each other trying to stay on those bucking and wild running animals. I climbed back up on the straw stack, but this time I had my mind made up. I was going to pick out one of the milk cows. They were not as agile as that young heifer. I lined up with the Guernsey milk cow, just below me as I lay down on my stomach on the edge of the straw stack. I thought this old milk cow would be an easy ride as I slid down, but when I landed and straddled her back, it scared her and she let out a bellow and away she went with me holding on with all my might. After about six seconds when she was making a high twisting buck, I was thrown into the grass again.

I was a little tired and thirsty, so I walked up to the well and got a drink. The livestock-watering tank has an eight-inch wide side to it, so I sat down on the side to watch the rodeo that my three brothers were putting on. I sat there for several minutes watching all of the excitement. About that time, here came Herbert on the old skinny Jersey cow. She was running full speed, straight for the gate that leads to the old milking barn. The gate was closed so about six feet from the gate she makes an immediate 180-degree turn, heading right back where she came from. She unloaded Herbert right there by the gate, on his back in ankle deep mud and cow manure. We are all laughing like crazy, except Herbert. He put on the best act of the day.

Herbert is the one that has the worst temper of us boys. Now he was really mad. But we could not stop laughing. Herbert finished first place, because he stayed on that cow longer than any of us. However, he would have been much happier had he fallen off out there on the grass instead of that ankle deep mud and cow manure. We all had a good time that afternoon and finished our rodeo before Dad got home.

OUR HOLSTEIN BULL

On July 1, 1932, we had some firecrackers for the Fourth of July celebration. I suggested to Eugene that we get one of those four-inch firecrackers and throw it in the barnyard where the old bull was standing over there by the barn.

"Well, Dale, that might be rather interesting. Why don't we go to the house and get one and try it," Eugene answered.

Now this big, I mean big, Holstein bull had gotten out of our pasture one time and gotten in the pasture with our neighbor's milk cows. Our neighbor Harry Bossomworth, just south of our pasture tried to get our bull separated from his cows. But this old bull wasn't about to leave, so Harry went home got his shotgun and gave that bull a load of buckshot right in the side. Some of the pellets were still buried under his skin. He wasted no time getting back through the fence just like he got out. He was aware of the excruciating pain after he heard that loud noise.

The bull was standing there by the red barn. We lit the firecracker and threw it out there between the water trough and the barn. As the firecracker fuse was burning and smoking, curiosity got the best of our bull, so he started slowly walking over to it. We thought he would leave rather than walk over to check it out. Just as he got there, put his nose down close and started sniffing to see what was that strange thing, the firecracker went off like a stick of dynamite.

That old bull let out a bellow and jumped about three feet into the air, as his feet hit the ground he was running full speed, kicking up a big cloud of dust. He never looked back. I was laughing about it, thinking, I am getting even for all the times you chased me. He ran to the far corner of the pasture, and then turned around to see if anything was following him.

I never thought he would come that close to the firecracker. I thought he might leave as soon as he saw us coming, but no. He got his nose almost on it.

Eugene said, "Yeah, he just got shot in the side with a shotgun a couple of days ago, he probable thought this is the end."

THE CORNCOB BATTLE

"Why don't we have a good old corncob fight, to create a little excitement," I suggested one afternoon.

"Yeah Dale, that sounds like a good idea. Better than standing here complaining about the weather," Eugene said.

Now this was a dreary, cloudy, Sunday afternoon in March 1933. Dad was not home so it was a good time to create a little excitement. The weapon of a good corncob fight is a peach limb about five feet long and about three quarters of an inch in diameter on one end and about one quarter of an inch in diameter on the other end, and sharpened. Then you get a corncob from the pigpen or there in the barnyard, where it has soaked good in barnyard waste. You break it in half, and stick the sharpened end of the peach limb into the pithy end of the corncob, good and tight. The peach limb should also be nice and limber, so you can give it a good quick snap at the end of the throw, and the corncob will fly off like streak of lightening and you hope that you have it aimed at someone.

This afternoon there were seven of us, the four of us boys and three of our neighbors, looking for something to do. Emmett Spangler was about my age, a stocky young boy with bright red hair. Forest Anderson was a slim wiry young man a little older than Eugene was. And Kenneth Lovett was a chunky young man about Virgil's age, a good sport but maybe a little slow on the uptake.

This game is not played by choosing sides. It is every man for himself. First, we went out to the peach orchard and got a good peach limb to launch the corncobs. Then, we all have one minute to get some good corncobs and a place to hide. There are two large barns, a garage, a smokehouse, two chicken houses, a brooder house for baby chickens, a machine shed, a granary, several hog houses, and three corncribs to hide behind. The object here is to hide from everyone else, but move around very cautiously, so no one sees you. Every few minutes you would hear someone hollering that they had been hit. Quite often, you would hear those wet cobs slam up against a building somewhere. Hopefully it was not close to you. I had a couple of shots that missed me, as I was sneaking around the corncribs and chicken house. Around the corncribs is a good place to be, there is plenty of ammunition.

The chicken house was close by, so very quietly I snuck over behind it. I peeped out around the south end of it just as Emmett stuck his head out from behind the pig house, which was close by. I was about 30 feet from him when I cut down on him with one of those wet, barnyard soaked corncobs. I gave that peach limb a quick snap just as I reached the end of my throw. That corncob flew off that peach limb full speed and hit him right behind the ear. His red hair stood up on end, he let out a scream, and fell down on the ground and did not move.

I ran over toward him, and screamed out, "I hit Emmett in the head, and I think I knocked him out."

About the time I got over to him he started to move and got up slowly, staggering around a little, and said, "Someone hit me in the head, right behind my ear. Did you do that?"

"I guess so, I am the only one here," I said. About that time, everyone else came running up hollering and asking what had happened.

"That little brother of yours hit me right in the head with one of those hog manure soaked corn cobs," Emmitt said.

They all asked, "Are you okay?"

"Oh I think so," Emmett said, still rubbing his head.

We stood around and talked about the near missed shots we had, and decided we would practice throwing at the buildings or any stray animals that came by, but not each other for the rest of the day. Someone might get hurt.

NOLA RAN INTO THE PORCH WITH THE 1926 FORD

"Dale, I want you and Eugene to go out to that forty acres of corn on the John Ragel place. You know where it is? You cultivated there just last week. Take a couple of corn knives and cut out all of the small stalks of corn. Do not leave more than two stalks in each hill. Also you better grab one of those water jugs on the back porch, and take some water with you," Dad instructed Eugene and me.

Eugene went to fill the water jug while I headed to the barn to get us a couple of good corn knives.

The water jug was a one-gallon jug with a cork in the end where you fill it and drink from. The cork was actually a corncob, but a clean one. The jug is wrapped with a burlap bag and twine string wrapped and tied in a way to hold the burlap bag in place. When you fill the jug you also soak the burlap with water, then the evaporation of the water keeps the drinking water nice and cool.

Dad asked Nola to take us boys out to the cornfield so she would know where to go and pick us up for dinner. He turned toward us boys and let us know he expected us to keep working until she got there to pick us up.

"We'll do the best we can, Dad," I answered. Nola got in the car, a 1926 Model T Ford coupe, and told us to put the corn knives and water jug on the floorboard and get in.

"Nola, are you sure you can drive this car," I asked.

"Yes," she said. "I have driven the Model T several times. You just get in and be quiet."

I did, but I watched every move she made to be sure she knew what she was doing. She started the engine, pushed in on the center pedal, and backed around to the driveway. Then she pushed in on the left pedal, which is low gear, and drove out onto the road and turned left. Then she pushed the emergency brake lever all the way forward, which was high gear. So I thought sure enough she knew how to drive this thing. I sat back and was quiet as she told me to do.

She drove through St. James and coming near the cross road, she asked, "Which way do I go here?"

I responded smartly, "You told me to be quiet."

"Don't be wise with me, Dale, or you will walk the rest of the way."

"Okay, Nola. You turn right and about a half a mile down the road on your left is a forty acre field of corn where we are going to work today."

Nola drove to the far side and pulled into the lane at the end of the cornfield. She said she would meet us there just before dinnertime. Nola also reminded us to thin out the corn just like Dad told us to. We thanked her for bringing us out there. Eugene and I got our drinking water and corn knives out of the car and got to work.

Here was this forty acres of bright green corn a quarter mile long and a quarter mile wide ahead of us. I told Eugene how Dad wanted us to leave only two stalks in each hill. I took the first two rows and Eugene took the next two. We started out on the quarter-mile trip to the other end. We were both barefooted, so we had to be careful that we did not whack our toes. When there were only two healthy stalks in the hill, I had no trouble cutting out the puny ones, but if there happened to be three healthy ones with the other little stalks, I did not want to cut the healthy stalks, it made me feel bad. I thought they would grow up to have big ears of corn, so sometimes I left three stalks if they were large and healthy. We soon got a rhythm to it, cutting out all of the little stalks in both rows and sometimes a big one if there were more than two. It wasn't long until we were at the far end of the field. We straightened up, got the kinks out of our backs, and headed back with four more rows, cutting out all but two healthy stalks most of the time. By the time we finished those eight rows, we had the system figured out, just bend over whacking one hill on our right and one on the left, moving forward all the time, almost in a slow walk. At the end of the field, we went over to the shade where we left our water jug, and got a good drink of that cool clear water. When you are hot, sweaty, and thirsty, that cool water sure tasted good.

We kept up this routine of thinning the corn from one end of the field to the other, getting the kinks out of our back and resting a few minutes at the far end of the field, then back to get a drink of that cool water and another short rest. After what seemed like several hours, we were getting close to the end of the field near the road. I told Eugene I was getting hungry. It seemed about dinnertime.

"I'm getting hungry too," he answered.

When we got to the end, and went to get another drink, we saw a car coming down the road and sure enough, it was that black Model T Ford.

Nola pulled into the lane at the end of the cornfield and called to us,

"Are you boys ready for dinner?"

I answered, "We have been ready for some time."

She told us to get our corn knives and water jug and hop in. When I laid the corn knives on the floor in the car, I did not like them there under our bare feet, I was afraid we might get our feet cut, so I laid them over to the left and up toward the front. The floorboards were sloping back a little, but the knives laid there okay. Nola pushed in on the reverse pedal and backed out of the lane onto the road. She pushed in on the low pedal and then pushed the emergency brake lever all the way forward for high gear and we were on our way home.

She drove all the way home with no problems. She made a right hand turn into the driveway, then another right turn heading for the side of the front porch, in the shade. All of a sudden, she hit the side of the porch. Wham!

Nola, all excited, said, "I couldn't push the brake pedal down!"

Dad came running out of the house asking, "What happened?"

Nola, rather nervous and upset, said, "I don't know, I couldn't push the brake pedal down."

I looked down on the floorboard, and exclaimed, "The corn knives have worked down under the brake pedal, and jammed the pedal so you couldn't push it down."

Dad said rather angrily, "Why in the world did you put the corn knives up there by the brake pedal anyway?"

"Well, we are both barefooted and I didn't want those sharp knives down here on the floorboard where they could cut our feet."

"Well, I don't want you to put them up there where they can get under the brake pedal again either," he said.

Dad pushed the car back from the porch a little and we all looked at the front end. It didn't look too bad as Dad took a hold of the front of the left fender and gave it a hard pull. That pretty well repaired all of the damage.

"Let's all go in and eat dinner," he said.

After dinner, Dad said he would take us back to work. Nola was still a little shook up from the accident, and he wanted to see what kind of a job we were doing, thinning out the corn. Eugene went to refill the water jug, being sure to wet the burlap around the jug real good so we would have cold water to drink in the afternoon. I went to get a burlap bag to put the corn knives in so we wouldn't cut our feet on them.

We all got in the Model T Ford and drove out to the cornfield. Dad drove to the lane at the far side of the field, pulled in, and parked. Eugene got the jug of water and put it under the shade tree, where it would stay nice and cool. I took the two corn knives out of the burlap bag as Dad was walking across the end of the field. The corn glistened in the hot summer sun.

"I think you left three stalks of corn in several of these hills," Dad pointed out.

"Well, Dad I only left three if they were large healthy stalks. I thought they would make three large ears of corn," I replied.

"No," he said, "this ground is not rich enough and we don't have any money to buy fertilizer. I want only two stalks left in each hill. You don't need to do this over because I want you to finish here this week."

We promised to only leave two stalks in each hill.

Dad said, "That is exactly what I want, but you need to finish this field by Saturday evening."

So we continued our routine of thinning the corn by cutting to the far end of the field, straightening up and giving our back a rest for a few minutes. Then back to the other end for a rest and drink of water. We continued this for the next five days and by Saturday evening, we had the forty acres of corn thinned out.

Footnote: Just to give you an idea of the size 40 acres is. It is a quarter mile by a quarter mile. One acre of corn in the Nineteen Thirties was 10 rows of corn, a quarter of a mile long, or 400 rows in 40 acres.

PLOWING DRY HARD GROUND

Dad asked Eugene and me, "Do you think you two could plow that south 40 of the 80 acres you kids got from Grandpa Stine?"

"I don't know Dad. When I plowed before, you always laid off the land by plowing the first round so we would have something to follow," I replied.

Dad said, "Okay, after breakfast we'll load the two walking plows onto those two wagons out there, and I'll go along with you to help unload the plows and get you started."

After breakfast, Eugene harnessed the team of horses, Dick and Blackie. Dick was a Morgan horse, built strong but very agile. Blackie was a very strong, black horse. They made a good team, capable of a lot of hard work. I harnessed the team of mules, Molly and Toby. They were the tallest and biggest team of mules in the county. We entered them in the County Fair and every year they took first place. They were also very gentle and good workers. In fact, Molly is the one that I put a firecracker under her tail, when Eugene and I were cultivating corn a few years ago. I hoped she had forgotten about that by now.

I hitched the team of mules up to one wagon and Eugene hitched his team of horses to the other wagon. Dad helped us load the walking plows, doubletrees, singletrees, and necessary clevises to hook the horses and mules to each plow. After we got everything loaded, Dad sent me to get the water jug and fill it with water from the well. I ran to the barn to get the jug and filled it with nice cool water. As I sat the jug in the wagon, Dad got in the wagon with me and set out to help us get started. He told me to turn the mules and wagon around that tree in the yard and head out toward the road.

You need to know how to stand up in the wagon. There is no seat, so you need to know how to keep your balance as the steel wheels on the wagon roll over the ruts and rough places in the road. With a practically empty wagon, we usually drive the horses or mules in a trot, which is about four to five miles an hour. We had about one and a half miles to travel to the field where we were going to plow. I tried to keep my balance as we bounced around over the dirt roads.

I will explain what a doubletree and singletree is, and how I hitch the mules to the walking plow. A doubletree is a crossbar with two singletrees attached to keep a team of two horses working together. It was a two by six piece of hickory or oak, about five feet long with a half-inch hole drilled in the center near the front. This makes the doubletree stronger when you attach the plow to the doubletree deep clevis. Then another clevis hook goes into that clevis, and the bolt end of the second clevis is attached to the plow beam by a double row of holes in the attachment on the plow beam. The plow beam has eight holes that are vertical to the plow. The higher you attach the doubletree to the plow the deeper the plow will go into the ground. Then, the singletrees are about 30 inches long with a hole in the middle, but toward the front side. This is attached to the doubletree with two clevises hooked together. There is a special singletree hook on each end of the singletree to hook to the mule's tugs.

As we approached the north end of the 40 acres to be drilled (planted) for wheat in October, Dad said, "Pull in the lane here and park the wagon over there under the shade tree."

As I pulled up under the shade tree, I asked Dad, "Is this okay here?"

"Sure. Let's unload the plows and everything right here in the nice cool shade of the tree," he answered.

After we had the plows and everything unloaded, I put the water jug in the cool grass up next to the tree trunk. Dad said, "Now I want you to unhitch the horses and mules from the wagons, and hitch them to the plows."

I unhitched the four tugs from the singletrees and unhitched the neck yoke from the mule's collars. The center of the neck yoke attached to the wagon tongue is what guides the wagon as the mules pull the wagon along with the tugs attached to the singletrees. I am sure this is all clear as mud. I hitched the mules to the walking plow, and Dad told Eugene to get the horses hitched to the plow, drag it over closer and he would show Eugene how to lay off the land.

"You head the horses to the other end of the field with the horse on your right to walk right in this dead furrow where I'm standing. This is the low place from where the land was plowed last year. Keep the horse on your right in this furrow, and make it straight all the way to the other end."

Eugene said, "Dad, I thought you were going the layoff (start) the land for us."

"I'm going to start the one for Dale, but you are older. Just watch how I start this land for Dale." Dad did the same thing with the mules on the next dead furrow over about 80 feet from where he started Eugene. Dad told Eugene, "You just watch how I start here and you do the same thing." Dad drove the mules about 20 feet and stopped. He said, "This ground is so dry and hard I can't hardly get the plow in the ground. Dale, you need to raise the doubletree up about two holes where it is attached to the beam on the plow."

I raised it up two holes.

Dad said, "Okay, I will see if I can get the plow in the ground now."

The plow went in the ground but the soil was so dry and hard it was plowing up in big chunks, some of them one and a half feet long by one foot wide. Dad was big and strong so he kept right on plowing and the mules were really pulling hard to pull the plow through that hard ground.

Eugene rose up the doubletree hitch on his plow two notches as Dad had done and tried it. The plow was knocking him around a lot but he just kept right on plowing. I waited there under the shade of the tree, until they came back. Dad turned the mules around and headed them back, with the mule on the right in the furrow that he plowed first.

"Okay, Dale, there you are. Have at it."

I answered, "I don't know, Dad. This ground is so hard. It looked like it knocked you around quite a lot."

"Yeah! You will get used to it after a couple of days," he answered. "Hitch the horses and mules back on the wagons about noon time so you can come in to water and feed the animals. And we will have a bite to eat also."

"That sounds good to me. I will do the best that I can."

I am usually excited and proud that I can do a new job on the farm but this looks like these plow handles could beat you black and blue as the large chunks of dry hard earth is turned over by the plow. But I will do my best, are my thoughts. I took the reins of the mules, put them over my shoulders, and grabbed those plow handles, which were right even with my ribs. I said, "Giddy up," to the team of mules and I was on my way. I held on to those plow handles with all my strength. Every time one of those big chunks of that dry hard earth turned over, that plow handle in my right hand would crack me a good one right in the ribs. This happened many times before I got to the other end of the field. It was the same thing on the way back. When we got to the end of the field, Eugene suggested we take a break and get some water. That sure sounded good to me. Besides those plow handles were really banging me around.

After we checked our sore ribs, got a drink of water, and rested a little while, I said, "We should wait until we get a good rain and plow this field then."

Eugene agreed that would sure be a lot easier than what we are trying to do now. We continued plowing for about four hours, stopping by the shade tree at the end of the field, to get a drink of cool clear water, and rest awhile in the cool shade of this large shade tree. The furrows we were plowing were in the north to south direction. I sighted down the furrow and the sun was just a little bit east of straight overhead.

I told Eugene, "Why don't we plow one more round then hitch these mules and horses to the wagons and go home for dinner?"

Eugene's answer was, "I am ready for dinner right now, but I guess you are right, we should plow one more round first."

Which we did, then we hitched the horses to the wagons. I set the water jug in my wagon, and we headed home for dinner and a short rest. I think the mules trotted a little faster going home, because they were hungry and thirsty also.

When we got home, we unhitched the mules and horses, and they headed right for the water trough. I asked Eugene if he would go feed the horses while I pumped water for them. Eugene put hay in their manger and some oats and grain in their feed box. Each horse had an individual manger and feed box and they knew exactly which stall was theirs. They headed right for it when they were through drinking.

As Eugene and I went into the house, Dad noted we got home almost exactly at noon for dinner, but wanted to know how the plowing was going. I told Dad the plow handles were beating me up, and my arms were sore trying to hold the plow handles upright when the hard chunks of dirt were being turned over. I asked if we couldn't wait until a good rain and plow it then. Dad was quick to say no. We needed to get it plowed now, so we could disk and harrow the field and get the ground ready to drill (plant) the wheat. I asked him if we could use the Fordson tractor. That tractor plows two furrows at a time so it wouldn't take long to plow the whole field. Dad said we did not have the money to buy fuel. He reminded me that the last hogs we sent to the St. Louis stock market didn't even sell for enough money to pay the freight to ship them down there. There was just no way to get any money. Therefore, we agreed to do the best we could. When we finished eating dinner, Dad went in the living room and sat down in his rocking chair beside the library table. Eugene and I went in the living room and laid down on the carpeted floor to rest. We went to sleep almost immediately. We were so tired from fighting that plow all morning.

It was not long until Dad decided we, and the horses, had rested long enough. It was time to get out there and get that plow back in the ground. It was quite clear that Dad was not going to wait for a rain, nor was he going to use the tractor to plow those 40 acres. We went out to the barn and hitched the horses and mules back up to the wagons. I filled the water jug with fresh cool, good tasting water from the well. We were on our way back to plowing. When we got out to the field, we hitched the horses up to our plows and went back to the same routine, wrestling with that walking plow to the far end of the field. Sometimes those big chunks of dry hard ground we were plowing up were almost half as big as I am. We stopped long enough at the far end of the field to stretch and get the kinks out of our sore back and muscles. Then the same routine back to the shade tree at the end of the field where we got a drink of that cool water and let the horses rest a couple of minutes, then back at it again.

Almost four weeks later, we completed plowing the 40 acres of dry, hard ground. As we completed the last furrow, I was sure glad to be finished. There for a while I didn't think we would ever see this last furrow completed.

Eugene breathed a sigh of relief and said, "I am sure glad it is over. This is the hardest job we ever had to do." I definitely agreed with that.

SHUCKING CORN

As we were eating breakfast, Dad informed us boys that because today is Saturday and we will all be home from school, we are going to go out to the John Simpson farm and shuck corn. Mr. Simpson's cornfield is two miles east of us in Effingham County and it will be a cold ride out there, as it is December 18, 1933. Once we start shucking corn, it will warm us up.

As we finished breakfast, Dad told us to go and put sideboards on all four sides of one wagon and two extra sideboards on the right side of the other wagon for a backboard. Then, go and harness the team of mules and the two horses for the other wagon. Virgil, Eugene, and I harnessed the horses and hitched them up to the wagons. Dad finished feeding the hogs and let the cows out to pasture.

Dad came over to the wagons and said, "I couldn't find a thing in the house to make for lunch. We ate that entire big pan of biscuits I made to go with our oatmeal for breakfast."

"Well, couldn't we go to the Simpson store right there where we will be shucking corn, to get something to eat," I asked.

"I thought about that. I have almost one dollar here in change in my coin purse. We could get a box of soda crackers, a stick of baloney and the rest of my money in bulk peanut butter," Dad said.

That sounded good to me, because I like baloney and peanut butter with crackers. Virgil and I went and filled the two jugs with water. The jugs had burlap bags wrapped around them to keep the water from freezing, with twine string to hold the burlap in place. Before we got in the wagon, Dad made sure we each had gloves and our shucking peg. The mules were hitched to the wagon Eugene and I rode in. Virgil and Dad were in the other wagon.

The shucking peg Dad reminded us about is a metal bar you hold in your hand to help with shucking the corn. The metal piece is wider than your hand and extends out to your thumb with a slight curve to fit your thumb. It has a leather strap with large loops to put your fingers through, even with your gloves on. You grab the shucks at the end of the ear of corn, rip the shucks open, and reach in and grab that ear of corn. As you hold the corn stalk tightly, just at the butt of the ear of corn, snap the ear out with your right hand and throw it up against the bump board on the far side of the wagon. If you over throw it you have to go and pick it up. However, if it don't make it into the wagon, whoever is shucking the two inside rows usually picks it up.

We drove the horses in a trot most of the two miles out there. The sun was not very high in the sky when we got to the field. Dad and Virgil pulled in on the right side of the first four rows. Eugene and I pulled our wagon on the last row that they had shucked and started in on the next four rows of corn. Shucking that corn one ear at a time takes a long time to get a wagonload. We shucked one round, which was eight rows for each wagon. The country store was at that end of the field, so we decided to stop early for lunch. When we walked up to the front door of the store, there was a sign on the door that read, "We have gone to our neighbor's funeral in Altamont. The store will be closed all day." We all let out a sigh of disappointment. My heart sank. I was sure looking forward to those soda crackers with baloney and peanut butter. We all looked at each other in amazement.

Dad's only comment was, "I guess we'll go back to shucking corn."

We went back to where we had left off, got our water jugs and had a drink of water and started back to work. Thank God, for the water.

Virgil and Dad took the first four rows, Eugene and I the next four rows, shucking the corn one ear at a time. We went another round of eight rows for each wagon. Dad looked up at that hazy sun and said, we could make one more round and get home before dark. We stopped long enough for another drink. The water was partly frozen, but it sure tasted good. Then we headed the horses and wagons back for one more round, four rows each way thru the field, shucking the corn, one ear at a time. When we finished that round, we were tired and hungry. Each one of us had shucked an equivalent of one row of corn three miles long!

We got home just before dark but still had to unload both loads of corn. Our scoop shovel had the handle broken, so Dad put in another handle he made from an old tree limb that had a slight bend to it. The scoop shovel had holes worn through the bottom, which made it very limber to try to scoop corn.

We scooped the corn into a rail crib. A rail crib is a three-sided corncrib made of rails, about four inches wide on each side, split from a log. You start out on a wooden platform, lay two rails on opposite sides of the platform, and then lay two rails on the adjacent sides, overlapping about six inches at each end. Then you just keep adding rails as you fill the crib with corn to as high as you want to scoop the corn. We switched off on the scooping and someone would help put on more rails when needed. If you were not scooping corn, you had to unharness the horses and feed them or milk the cows and feed them and feed the hogs.

Dad went into the house to get something for dinner. When we got all the farm chores finished, we went in to wash up for dinner. When I sat down at the table, there were plates and silverware for all four of us, and two large bowls in the middle of the table, with what looked like rice to me. I noticed no one had started eating, so I started in on the rice. I noticed everyone looked at me rather funny as I took a large helping. It was not rice. It was cooked turnips. I did not like turnips at all because that had been our main diet that winter. None of us boys liked turnips. Dad had fooled me. I thought it was rice. Since we were all very hungry we ate all of the turnips and had milk to drink. I do not like cooked turnips to this day.

HERBERT'S ACCIDENT WITH THE FORDSON TRACTOR

Just as we were about to sit down to dinner, Mr. Miller rushed over with urgent news. Herbert had just turned the tractor over and he was bleeding very badly from a cut on his left arm. Dad rushed out the back door all excited and asked what had happened.

Bill Miller who had just driven up in his pickup truck said, "Herbert just turned the tractor over in the road, just past your hedge row, he is bleeding real bad. You better get something for a tourniquet to stop the bleeding and get him to the doctor right now."

Mr. Miller went back with his son-in-law, Clyde, to try to stop the bleeding. Dad told us to just push the dinner on the back of the stove for now and jump in the car. He went and got a towel to use for a tourniquet and we headed down to see what we could do. We all piled in the car.

Virgil said, "I wonder how he could have turned the tractor over in the road."

Dad said, "I don't know, but if it can be done one of you boys will figure out how to do it."

We drove up to where the accident happened and sure enough, the tractor was sitting there with all four wheels up in the air. They had Herbert out from under the tractor and used his shirtsleeve to make a tourniquet. His arm was all bloody and he had a deep cut from his elbow to his shoulder. I was scared after seeing all that blood and I was afraid he was going to lose his arm.

As Dad was wiping the blood off Herbert with the towel, he said, "How in the world did you turn this tractor upside down right here in the middle of the road?"

As Dad put the bloody towel on his arm for a better tourniquet, Herbert said, "I don't know, I was just coming home for dinner, I guess the front wheels got caught in that rut, and jerked the steering wheel out of my hand, and the front wheels turned sharp to the left, and just rolled this thing upside down. But my arm is sure hurting."

Dad got him in the car and headed off in a shot for Dr. Whiteford in St. Elmo to see if he could get Herbert fixed up. As they drove off I said, "It is a wonder that he didn't get killed or at least cut up more than he did."

We had just taken the rear fenders off to have them welded. The fenders would have protected him from the rear wheels, but they were in the welding shop.

Bill Miller asked, Virgil, "Do you think the five of us could turn this tractor up on its wheels again?"

"Well, we won't know unless we try, will we?"

We all got over on the other side of the tractor, got a good solid place to lift, and pushed on the tractor to get it back on the wheels. Virgil said for us to give it our best effort, and lift with all of our strength. We lifted it up to the point where it was balanced, and gave it a little push. Right up on the wheels it went. I thanked Bill and Clyde for helping us, and taking care of Herbert until we got there.

Virgil was the oldest of us boys that were there and he looked the tractor over, thought everything seemed to be okay, and tried to crank it. After cranking two or three times, it started up. He got on the tractor and drove it home.

As Eugene and I were walking home, we hoped that Herbert's arm would be okay, but all of that blood made us afraid they might have to amputate his arm. We talked about Herbert and how could he turn the tractor over just driving it down the road. As Eugene and I walked in the yard, Virgil came out from behind the garage. He said the tractor seemed to run perfectly all the way home.

I think Herbert was sure lucky only getting his arm cut, sitting down there between those two big wheels, with those big cleats on the wheels whirling close by his head. With the tractor in road gear, it must be doing twenty miles an hour or more. Without those fenders on there, it sure looked dangerous to me.

That afternoon when Dad and Herbert came home, I ran out to the car to see how Herbert was.

"What did the doctor do to you," I asked.

Herbert said he had seventeen stitches in his arm. Herbert continued, "And that hurt worse than when the tractor wheel ripped my arm from my elbow up almost to my shoulder."

Dad said we were lucky Herbert didn't get hurt any worse than he was.

With all of the excitement, we realized we hadn't had dinner yet and by then it was midafternoon. Dad rubbed his stomach and sent us boys to be washed up while he put the still warm soup beans and ham on the table.

I asked to go down in the cellar and get one of those half-gallon fruit jars of canned blackberries, which we picked and canned last summer. That sounded good to Dad so I rushed to get one. We all sat down to a good home cooked meal, no cooked turnips.

First thing the next morning, Dad headed over to the welding shop to get the fenders, and put them back on the tractor before anyone else drove the tractor.

REPLACING THE BRAKES ON OUR 1929 CHEVROLET

As Dad drove in the driveway, he got out of the car and said, "There is something terribly wrong with these brakes. The car pulls hard to the right every time I use the brakes, and there is a horrible clanging noise under the front end."

I said, "Yeah, I heard all of that grinding and scraping noise as you were coming in the driveway. As soon as I take this milk into the milk house, I will come back and take a look under the car to see if I can see if anything is wrong." I looked under the right front end of the car because Dad said it was pulling hard to the right. I looked hard at the brake lines, the brake drum, and steering rods. Everything looked okay to me. I went over and looked under the left front of the car. The first thing I looked at was the brake drum and it looked like it was cut in half, around the circumference of the drum. I got under the car and looked real close and sure enough, the outside of the drum was separated from the part attached to the wheel. It was just clanging around under the car.

I went out the where Dad was feeding the hogs and told him what the brake drum looked like.

He said, "When Virgil gets home from cultivating corn I will have him go look at it also. Why don't you go and finish the milking and I will feed the cows here in the red barn. Virgil should be home by then."

I went and got the two milk buckets and finished the milking. I was more interested in what happened to the brake drum on the car. I milk cows every night and morning, but I seldom get a chance to help work on the cars or tractor.

Virgil came in from cultivating corn, and had the horses watered, fed and unharnessed, by that time I finished milking. As I went to strain the milk, I stopped and told Virgil what happened to the brake drum on the car.

I said, "Why don't you jack up the left front wheel of the car, while I go and strain this milk. Then we will take the wheel off and see what is wrong." I was curious as to what caused the brake drum to split in half.

After I finished with the milk, I went back out to the car. Virgil had the car jacked up and was taking the lug nuts off.

About that time, Dad walked up and said, "I thought we would wait until morning to look at the car, when it is daylight."

Virgil said, "Dale was all excited about what had caused the brake drum to split like that, so I went and got the lantern, so we could see how to remove the wheel."

We got the wheel off. The brake drum was a big problem. The brake shoes were a mess. And the brake lining is completely worn off and the metal that the brake lining is riveted to is all worn off. The heavy metal rib that is the strength to the brake shoes, had just worn or cut through the circumference of the drum, which caused the inner half to fall off and clang around in there as the wheel turned.

Dad looked at all of the broken and worn brake parts and said, "Why don't you get all of these broken parts off of there and put that wheel back on, so we can go to the auto junk yard in Altamont tomorrow and get a good brake drum and front brake shoes off of a '29 Chevrolet."

I said, "Dad, can you drive the car without brakes on the left front wheel?"

"Yeah, I have been driving it for about a year with all of that grinding noise. We didn't have any money to buy new brake shoes, so I just kept driving it."

I just graduated from the 7th grade, and school was out for the summer. I was all excited about going to the junkyard in the morning with Dad and Virgil. They have all kinds of old wrecked cars there that I could study. That will be great fun.

The next morning we had the chores all done and finished breakfast. Dad told Virgil, "You and Dale get the tools that we will need to take the brake shoes and drum off of the car at the junk yard."

We got the jack and wrenches we needed to do the job and put them on the floorboard in the back seat.

I went into the house and told Dad, "We have all the tools in the car and we are ready to go."

Dad's answer was, "Okay, I will be right out."

In no time, we were all in the car and headed for the junk yard.

Dad said, "The brakes are about the same. It pulls to the right but I don't hear all of that scraping and clunking noise. But the steering seems awful loose, like I turn the steering wheel a lot to get the car to change direction."

Virgil said, "When I took that wheel off I noticed the kingpins were awful loose, so why don't we get a new set of kingpins. I can install them at the same time we are fixing the brakes."

"If I have enough money left after we get the brake parts, we will do that," was Dad's reply.

It was not long until we pulled into the junkyard and that is exactly what it looked like. We got out of the car and went inside.

The old man with about a 3-week growth of whiskers, behind the counter drawls out, "What can I do for you today?"

Virgil speaks up, "We need a brake drum and brake shoes for a 1929 Chevrolet."

He answered with, "I got a bunch of Chevys out there. Follow me and I will show you where they are."

As we walked along he said, "I am sure there is three or four 1929 Chevys there. Just take your pick."

Dad asked him, "How much does the brake drum and shoes cost?"

"Oh, I don't know maybe 50 cents to a dollar."

Dad answered, "I don't think they are worth more than 50 cents."

"Well, when you get them off bring them up to the counter, we will work something out."

Virgil and I were already on a dead run out to get the tools. I thought this was much more exciting than going to school or cultivating corn. We were going to tear that Chevy apart.

When we got back up to where the Chevys were parked Virgil said, "I think this green one here looks good. It should have a good brake drum and brake shoes. And the front of the car is easy to get to."

I told Virgil, "You loosen the lug nuts and I will jack the car up."

We got the wheel and brake drum off and everything looked good.

Dad's comment to that was, "They look so good. Why don't you take those brake shoes off, then remove the other front wheel, and get those brake shoes also."

That is what we did. We put both of the wheels back on the car so we could get the jack out from underneath the car. We gathered up our tools and car parts and went back up to the office, and laid the parts on the counter.

"Well, I think those parts are worth a dollar don't you?"

Dad's answer was, "My oldest son works for our neighbor on the farm from daylight to dark for $1 a day. I think those parts are worth about a half days labor, don't you?"

"Okay, I guess you have a good point there. Give me the 50 cents."

Dad put two quarters on the counter and said, "Thank you."

We picked up our parts and loaded them and the tools on the floor of the back seat.

As we drove off, Dad said, "I guess we better go by the Western Auto parts store and see if I have enough money to buy those kingpins."

We stopped at the Western Auto store in St. Elmo on our way home. We all got out of the car and went in. The parts stores always have many interesting things to look at. Dad told the man behind the counter we needed a set of kingpins for a 1929 Chevrolet.

"Okay, I will check the number and see if we have any in stock."

He wrote the number on a piece of paper and went back into the rows of shelves. In a minute or so he came out with a small box in his hand and said, "This is the last set I have. I will check the price for you." After thumbing through the price list, he stated, "They are a dollar a set. That is for the kingpins and bushings."

Dad took his coin purse out of his pocket and there was one-dollar bill in it. He gave it to the man. He said that as long as we were fixing the brakes, we should fix the steering too. I picked up the box and we all got back in the car and headed home. On the way Dad pointed out that now is when all the work starts; getting all of these parts installed on the car. We pulled in the driveway and Dad had me open the garage door so he could put the car in the garage to do the work.

"Let's go and get some of those six by six blocks we had left from building the red barn, to put under the front end of the car", Virgil said.

"That sounds like a good idea."

We were off to get the blocks. When we got back to the garage, Virgil had me get the jack and jack up the front of the car while he took off the lug nuts. Then we removed the brake drums and shoes. We could tell that the kingpins were really worn out because the wheel spindle was very loose; a sloppy fit on the kingpin. I removed the nuts on the anchor bolts and used a hammer to get the anchor bolts and the kingpins, which was the easy part. Virgil told me to get the new bushings and kingpins and oil them up real good. He cleaned up the yoke part of the wheel spindle. Then Virgil pushed the top and bottom bushing in each wheel spindle yoke.

I said, "Virgil, why don't we see if these kingpins will fit in the bushing, now that they are pressed in the yoke."

Sure enough, they would not fit.

I asked Virgil, "What are we going to do now?"

He answered, "We don't have any reamers. Why don't you go and get Dad, and he might have a suggestion."

Dad was working in the garden. I told him our problem.

He said, "Okay, I will come and look at it."

Dad tried everything he could think of but the kingpin would not even start into the bushing. Dad's comment was, "I don't know of any one that can ream those bushings. I guess you will just have to get a bigger hammer."

Virgil asked me to oil the kingpins and bushings again, while he went to look for the biggest hammer he could find. He came back with a big blacksmiths hammer and a sledgehammer. We put the upper end of the spindle yoke in the vise, and finally got the kingpin started, and with the big hammer drove it through the bushing.

About that time, Dad came out and said, "It will soon be dark so you better quit and milk the cows, and do the evening chores. You can finish this tomorrow." I was quite disgusted that we were having so much trouble installing the kingpins, and was not happy about having to quit, and go milk the cows again.

The next morning after morning chores were finished, right after breakfast, we were out in the garage. I had lost a little of my enthusiasm with this entire kingpin problem. With the big hammer and sledgehammer, we finally had the kingpins, locking bolts and the steering rods installed. It was almost impossible to turn the steering wheel.

I asked Virgil, "Do you think you are strong enough to drive this thing."

He replied, "I don't know, but we will keep greasing the kin pins and turning the steering wheel from side to side. Maybe it will get a little easier to turn."

We finally finished the job with the brake shoes and drums, adjusted the brakes, and installed the front wheels. Virgil got in the car and started it.

He said, "If I don't have to change directions, I won't have any trouble."

He backed it out of the garage, then pulled forward and backward a couple of times and said, "The brakes are very good but I don't know about the steering."

Dad heard the engine running so he came out to see if he could drive the car. He asked Virgil, "What do you think?"

"Well," Virgil said, "the brakes are excellent, but the steering is almost impossible."

Dad asked if he could try it, so he got in drove it back and forth a few times, trying the brakes and the steering. He said, "It drives like a big truck. I hope we don't have to make any quick changes of direction, because it's almost impossible to turn the steering wheel; but the brakes are great." This was a typical farm repair for 1934.

GRADE SCHOOL DAYS

I remember all of my grade school teachers very distinctly. My first and second grade teacher was Fairy Stine. She was strict, but was very kind to all of the students that were obedient. She lived in the first house west of us, just a little over a quarter of a mile away. When I was in the second grade, if the dirt roads were drivable, she would give me a ride to school in her shiny new Model A Ford Roadster. I felt really proud about getting to ride to school in her new car. There was a mud hole in the road between her house and ours that you couldn't get through in a car during most of the winter and early spring. The two or three times I got a ride to school, I thought I was really doing something to get to ride to school with the teacher.

My third and fourth grade teacher was Clint Mattox. Now he was entirely different from Fairy Stine. If you weren't doing schoolwork all the time, or if he saw you whisper to someone next to you or pass them a note, he would grab a piece of chalk or blackboard eraser and throw it at you. Sometimes he even threw the metal bell at you if he could not reach anything else.

This metal bell had a plunger on top that when you tapped it, it would cause the arm to strike the bell from the inside. The teacher rang the bell to start school in the morning, and to start or finish break or lunch period.

He also used his belt on the bigger boys if they were getting out of control. I remember him using the belt on my brother, Herbert, and on Wilson Lovett. He took them over by the heating stove, which was in the right rear corner of this one room schoolhouse. He took his belt off and really laid it on them. I was really scared. I was not about to do anything that might get me into trouble.

At recess or the noon lunch break, after we ate our lunch, we would go outside and play. Sometimes the boys played leapfrog. The ones that wanted to play would all line up. The person in front would bend over and the person behind him would put his hands on the back of the one bent over and straddling him, jump over, and crouch down becoming the front player. Then, the third person in line would jump over both of them, one at a time. They kept this up until everyone had jumped, then the last person in line would jump over all of them. This was a continuous line with the last person in line jumping over everyone in front of him. It was good exercise and we kept it up until someone got tired or it was time to go back into class. We also played Andy Over. You would choose two team captains, and then they would start choosing team players from the remaining students. Usually everyone wanted to play. The two captains usually choose the ones that could catch the ball the best first, then keep choosing until everyone was on one side or the other. Then each team got on the opposite sides of the schoolhouse. We had a soft sponge or rubber ball that the chosen side would throw over the top of the schoolhouse, yelling "Andy Over." If the opposite side caught the ball they would say, "Andy Over, Andy Over, let Ronald come over," or the name of any other player on the opposite side. If they did not catch the ball, they threw it back over the schoolhouse, to see if the first team could catch the ball. We kept this up until all players were on one side of the schoolhouse and that team was the winner. We also played softball at noon and recess, using the backside of the schoolhouse for a backstop. I liked playing softball because it was a competitive sport. We never had enough players to have two teams. We played what we called Rounds In. If you were batting and struck out, you went to the outfield and every one moved up one place. If you were the catcher, you now became a batter, and so on until everyone has to play in all of the positions, which made it more exciting. Everyone wanted to bat.

My fifth and seventh grade teacher was Mary Fristoe. She was very jolly and good-natured and I enjoyed going to school when she was the teacher. The reason I had the fifth and seventh grade in succession is that the year I was supposed to take the sixth grade they decided to teach only four grades per year instead of all eight grades in the one-room country schools. From the fifth grade, I was promoted to the seventh grade, and then the next year I would be promoted to either the sixth or the eighth grade, depending on my grades. I made good grades in the seventh grade so was moved up to the eighth grade. I was excited and quite happy about that. I guess Mary Fristoe did a good job of teaching me. I liked her as a teacher and I think you naturally try harder to make better grades when you like the teacher.

My eighth grade teacher was Keith Stine. Now, all of the Stines and Ragels are related. His grandpa and my Grandpa Stine were brothers. Keith was a very good teacher; just out of college. He made sure you did all of your school assignments and encouraged you to do your very best. I made good grades, especially in arithmetic and spelling, and graduated from the eighth grade on April 27, 1934, with a certificate to attend any High School in the state of Illinois.

Keith also played softball with us. He pitched quite a lot to teach us to be good batters. I especially remember one day when he was pitching and I was the catcher. Keith was six feet tall and very muscular. He pitched very fast. The batter took a swing at the ball and just tipped it so it came up and hit me right in the nose and mouth. That really hurt! I spit blood for a while. I was not very anxious to be the catcher after that. We never had a facemask or shin guards, in fact, the catcher and first baseman were the only players that even had a glove. Sometimes, we would have a contest to see who could throw the ball the farthest. We had to stand behind home plate and then someone was a judge out in the field to mark where each ball stopped. I still like to play softball.

TRAIN WHISTLE

It was a cold winter night, December 12, 1935, and I was sleeping on the one-foot wide wooden ticket counter in the train depot in St. Elmo, Illinois. I heard that shrill train whistle coming in from the north and slid off that ticket counter, yelling, "Whoopee!"

The train had finally arrived to take us back to St. James. The reason we were in the train depot was that the dirt road from St. Elmo to St. James had several mud holes and a steep hill. During most of the winter, cars could not drive on the road unless it was frozen solid enough to support the weight of the car.

The St. James Basketball Team, all six of us and the coach, went to Mattoon, Illinois, in the coach's Model A Ford, which is how we went to all of the games. However, that night we had taken the train. Mattoon had a population of about 12,000. The gymnasium had a beautiful wood floor, whereas St. James had 17 houses, and a dirt basketball court. There were only nine boys in St. James, a three-year high school.

We were all in very high spirits that night as we had just beaten

Mattoon's second team 28 to 24. Everyone was charged up over the game. Matoon was over confident that they could beat a bunch of farm kids from a three-year high school that played on a dirt court.

We stayed and watched the main game that night, which was Mattoon against Decatur, two major cities in south central Illinois. I do not remember who won that game, but I saw several Mattoon players on the first team that played against us part of the time. I noticed that they had about fifteen players that they kept rotating into the game. That made us feel that much better that we won the game against some of their first team players.

As the train stopped in front of the depot, we all ran out and jumped aboard; we were on our way to St. James. During the five-mile journey, we recounted all of the good plays we had made in that game. That was one of the best games of the year. In no time at all we heard that shrill train whistle again as we approached the St. James depot. As we were getting off the train, Charlie Strough asked me to have breakfast with him so I didn't have to walk all the way home in the cold and right back to school again. That sounded good to me. I have not slept on any train depot ticket counter since.

STRUCK BY LIGHTNING

As we finished eating breakfast Dad asked me to harness up Beauty and Blackie and start cultivating corn on the north forty acres that Grandpa Stine had left to the grandchildren. I pleaded to use the riding cultivator because that old walking cultivator wore me out. Dad agreed I was big enough now to use the riding cultivator. That made me feel good.

I went out in the barn and harnessed Beauty. She was a good riding horse that I rode a lot so we were good friends. Then I harnessed Blackie. He is an old strong workhorse that can work all day long every day. I got them harnessed and hitched to the riding cultivator. Dad came over to make sure I was ready and reminded me to get a jug of water. I did not want to forget that. I went and filled the jug with cool clear water from the well. As I got on the cultivator to leave, Dad said to be sure and come in about noon to rest, get something to eat, and give the horses a little rest. It was a little cloudy and if the sun isn't shining, I can't tell when it is exactly noon.

Dad said, "When you get really awfully hungry, it is about noon."

"Okay Dad. I will figure it out," I replied. I got my jug of water and was on my way. It was about one and a half miles to the cornfield. When we got there, I stopped the horses and put the jug of water under the shade tree at the end of the field.

I started in on the first row of corn and I was feeling good that I got to cultivate corn with the riding cultivator. That was fun, doing it all by myself. I just had to watch that I didn't plow out any of the corn. I had two lines to guide the horse and I had them tied together and over my shoulder. I just had to turn them around at each end of the field. When you got them on each side of the row of corn, they know what they are supposed to do and seldom need correcting.

It was cool and cloudy that morning. I only had to stop to let the horses rest about every other round. I also got a drink of the good cool water. It sure tasted good. After about two hours, the sky was starting to get very dark and cloudy, and the wind was picking up. I thought that maybe I ought to go home because it looked like we might get a big rainstorm. Dad never quit working in the field until it rained very hard, so I kept right on cultivating that corn.

Dad never quit working in the field until it rained very hard, so I kept right on cultivating that corn.

Then it started to thunder and lightning. I was scared. It started to rain very hard, so as soon as I got to the end of the field I drove the horses out to the road. It was raining really hard now. The thundering and lightening was loud. I turned the horses south to Henry and Louise Smith's house, which was about a hundred yards down the road. There were two rows of big maple trees down each side of the driveway. I was going down the driveway and pulled back on the line to stop the horses. A streak of lightening hit one of the trees. I don't know if the lightening also struck me or not, but it sure was close. The rain was coming down like sheets of water and I was scared. I had a horrible excruciating pain in my right eye, my artificial eye. The eye is concave shaped and hollow. I held my hand over my right eye and went to the door. Louise was there to meet me. She had the door open hollering to get in out of the rain. Then she saw the blood running out from beneath my hand. She asked was I hurt and saw blood coming from under my hand.

"You are bleeding!"

I told her about the lightning striking the tree in the driveway and the immediate sharp pain in my right eye. She helped me wash my hands in the washbasin on the porch. I wanted to remove the artificial eye so she could take a better look.

"You are bleeding badly from your right eye," she said.

After I got my hands washed and dried I tried to remove my eye, but it seemed like there was suction holding my eye in the socket. There were sharp pieces of glass piercing the eye socket, which was very painful. I finally got it loose and removed the front part of the eye, and then most of the pain was gone. Louise looked into my eye. There were several broken pieces from the backside of my artificial eye still in there. She brought some fresh water to try to wash out the broken pieces of glass. She got several pieces out, looked into my eye, and when she didn't see any more glass, she asked me to blink a few times. I did and there was no more serious pain. I thanked her for getting all of the glass out of my eye. I felt much better and thought I should be headed home.

She was going to put a bandage on my eye but I protested. I didn't need one, but she went to get some gauze and tape anyway. She put the bandage on my eye and gave me a little hug. She offered me a glass of milk and a peanut butter and jelly sandwich. I said that I wasn't really hungry and I needed to get home. She went right ahead, made me a sandwich anyway, and brought a glass of milk. I was glad she did because it was now noon or later and I was really hungry. It sure tasted good. I hated for her to go to all the trouble, but I was thankful she cleaned up my eye and now it felt much better.

She wrapped the outer piece of my eyeball in a piece of cloth and I put it in my shirt pocket and went home. By then the rain had stopped. As I went out the door, she gave me another little hug and I thanked her again.

THRESHING WHEAT

It was July 18, 1936, and my Uncle Sterl just pulled into the driveway with his International 15-30 tractor pulling the threshing machine. He got off the tractor and met Dad and me as we were coming out of the house. Dad showed him where he wanted the straw stack this year, just east of the red barn. Uncle Sterl pulled the threshing machine and set it so the tractor and the bundle wagon were up wind from the threshing machine. Then my uncle proceeded to line up the tractor about 50 feet in front of the threshing machine. There is a 100 foot belt about 8 inches wide that goes from the tractor drive pulley to the front left side of the threshing machine's input pulley. While my uncle was doing that, Dad sent me to hitch the mules up to the hay frame wagon and go up to the wheat field on the Lovett farm. I had helped shock the wheat there last month. When I got there, Sam Fristoe and Gus Durham were already loading Roy Smith's wagon. In a few minutes, Gerald Stine and Nelson Stine showed up with their wagons and Forest Anderson and Henry Schwarms came along to pitch the bundles up on the wagons. Forest and Henry pitched bundles up to load my wagon and we had it loaded in no time.

The stocks of wheat were all in a row so you just headed the mules down the row. After they pitch up the bundles from one shock you just say "giddy up" to the mules and say "whoa" when they get to the next shock. These mules have done this many times, so they know just exactly what to do.

When you are loading a bundle wagon, you place the bundles down each side of the wagon with the butt end out about six inches past the edge of the hay frame. The hay frame wagon has a rack about six feet tall in the front and back to hold the bundles in place. You place the bundles crossways in the wagon to help bind the load together. It also keeps the load somewhat level. You stop when you get the load about six or eight feet above the hay frame, or where you feel comfortable. You don't want it too high because you have to cross a ditch or two to get out of the field. And it is about one and half miles to the threshing machine.

Forest and Henry were pitching up the bundles quite rapidly, which really kept me busy loading them properly. The second row of bundles had to be placed crossways to tie the load all together and you had to keep the sides of the load higher so the bundles would always be slanting slightly to the middle of the wagon. It was not long until they had me about loaded.

I told Forest, "As soon as we get to the end of this row of shocks I am going to call it a load."

However, Forest said we could put on about a half dozen more shocks. I didn't want to take a load so big that I might dump the whole load crossing that ditch getting out onto the road. Henry agreed. Henry didn't want to pitch the whole load back up on the wagon a second time. I drove away with my wagon full.

I got across the ditch without any problems. As I got home, Uncle

Sterl motioned me to go out behind the tractor and pull up to the other side of the threshing machine where they are already threshing. Roy Smith was about half-unloaded. Some horses are mighty skittish when pulling up next to the running threshing machine. There is a lot of noise with all that machinery running, almost like a freight train coming into town. These mules have been there many times, so it did not bother them.

You put the bundles into the feeder trough length wise with the heads of the wheat in first. There is a double chain link conveyor with wood slats fastened to each side of the chain links. This carries the bundles into the threshing machine, where a set of four curved knives on the crankshaft turns very fast and cuts the binder twine that holds the wheat in bundles.

It takes a lot more people to do the grain threshing. It takes three or four to run the grain wagons, and they help to adjust the straw pipe and hood to form a semicircle straw stack. We borrowed one grain wagon from my Uncle Wes Ragel, which is grain tight and we just run the grain loose into the wagon. Then we scoop it from the wagon to the upstairs in the granary. Scooping the grain into the granary is a very hot and backbreaking job. Our wagon was not grain tight so we needed to sack all of the grain as it comes down the grain pipe into canvas or burlap bags. These bags hold about 100 pounds of wheat and are then dumped in the downstairs section of the grainery. It is a hot and backbreaking job.

When we were threshing, we also needed help in the kitchen to prepare lunch midmorning and midafternoon, with a very large and nourishing dinner at noon for about 20 people. My Dad's sister, Aunt Esther, and one of her daughters and three or four of the neighbor women prepared the lunches and dinner with plenty of iced tea and lemonade for everybody.

It did not take me very long to unload the wheat bundles into the threshing machine. As I pulled away, there was another wagon waiting to unload. On my way back to the wheat field, I stopped by the water pump in the barnyard to get a nice cool drink of water, right from the bottom of the well.

Back at the wheat field, Fristoe and Gus Durham pitched the bundles up on my wagon. I was busy getting the outside row and the next row overlapping enough to tie the outside bundles. They were pitching the bundles so fast I didn't have time to place them exactly. I had to let them fill the middle of the load, but you need to keep the outside rows the highest, to make the load solid, so it doesn't slide off the wagon going over rough ground. About the time I had a good half of a load, Gus started throwing up bundles two at a time. I told Gus to just pitch them up one at a time. No answer. I tried to put some in the middle and keep the sides up and straight but the bundles were piling up on me, so I just kicked about half a dozen bundles off the wagon back on the ground. Gus spoke little English, and when he got excited he usually talked in German. He ripped off something in German that I could not understand. I think he said he did not want to pitch the bundles twice.

"That's okay Gus," I called back to him, "just pitch them up one at a time."

He answered back something I still did not understand, but he started pitching up the bundles one at a time.

When I got the load up to a good seven feet high, I decided that was enough for this load and saw someone coming with iced tea and lunch. It was one of the cooks, driving our 1935 Chevrolet. I crossed the ditch and headed out onto the road. When I got home, they had shut down for lunch. I went into the kitchen and Aunt Esther gave me a couple of sandwiches, a piece of chocolate pie, and a nice ice-cold glass of tea. I was ready for that, especially the ice-cold tea. I was a growing boy of fifteen so it was no problem for me to put away two sandwiches and a piece of pie. About that time, I heard the tractor start up so I went out and drove out to the threshing machine, right up next to the feeder trough. I began throwing the wheat bundles into the cavernous mouth of that giant whirling and shaking machine, with those four curved knives whirling in thin air until you threw wheat bundles into the mouth to satisfy its ravenous appetite for more bundles of wheat.

It was not long until Nelson Stine pulled up on the other side of the feeder trough to help feed this ravenous machine. However, you must always put the bundles in head first, and you cannot feed it too fast or all of the straw will choke up inside the threshing machine. We kept up this routine until dinnertime when we unhitched the horses, watered, and fed them. This is the best part of threshing; you always had a very good meal, with all you could eat. There was desert and plenty of iced tea. This was especially a good treat for me, because my Mother had died when I was on one and a half years old and my stepmother, who was very good to all of us children, left when I was ten years old. So with four boys and Dad at home, during the great depression, good meals were few and far between, sometimes non-existent.

All of these farmers were helping us to thresh our grain. We had already helped them, or would help them when they threshed their grain. I always volunteer for that job. The routine is about the same every day for about a week as we usually have sixty to eighty acres of wheat and twenty to 30 acres of oats to thresh. The next day we finished the wheat on the Lovett farm and started on the sixty acres of the Jim Smith farm just south of us.

That afternoon the threshing machine broke, so everything stopped. Virgil came over to help Uncle Sterl and Gerald try to find out what broke.

They took the broken part off and Uncle Sterl went to the house to use our phone to call the International dealer in St. Peter.

He had to call the switchboard in St. James and they connected him to the International dealer in St. Peter. In a few minutes, Uncle Sterl came out of the house and said they have the part. He turned to Virgil and said, "You are the wildest and fasted driver around. You can get to St. Peter and back quicker than anyone else can. Will you go get the part?"

Virgil was already in the car with the engine running. Uncle Sterl didn't have the door shut before there were two rooster tails of dirt coming off both rear wheels as Virgil made a U-turn around the tree in the front yard, and out to the road in a cloud of dust. Everyone had a good laugh about Virgil's quick exit out of the yard.

Aunt Esther came out on the side porch and called us in for lunch with plenty of food, desert, and iced tea. That sounded good to me. We weren't even through with lunch when I heard a car drive in. I went out to see if they got the part.

I saw the car there in the front yard with blood and guts all over the windshield and front of the car. Virgil explained that on the paved section from Loogootee to St. Peter he had the car floor boarded, going over eighty miles per hour. There were some birds down the road, and he caught the rear end of a turtledove right on the hood ornament and blood and guts went everywhere.

Now that all the excitement was over, Virgil and Gerald put the new part on the threshing machine. Uncle Sterl started the tractor to see if the threshing machine was working. Everything seemed just fine and we were back to the threshing routine for three more days.

FILLING THE SILO

It was August 12, 1936, and silo filling time again. My brothers, Virgil and Eugene, and I were out in the barns, hog house, and chicken house doing the early morning farm chores. We had to milk and feed the cows, feed the horses, sheep, hogs, and chickens. Just as we finished working, Dad came out on the back porch and called us to breakfast. When we came to the back steps of the house Dad set out a wash pan, soap, and hung a towel by it.

"You boys wash up good before you come in for breakfast. I've fixed a big pan of hot biscuits with bacon and eggs," Dad said.

Hot biscuits! Bacon and eggs! What is the big occasion I wondered? Dad told us we were going out to help cut those twenty acres of corn to fill the silo today. I knew we were filling the silo today but I thought it would be the usual breakfast of oatmeal or cornflakes and milk. The four of us wolfed down all of those biscuits, with homemade butter, bacon, and eggs in no time. That breakfast sure tasted good.

Dad sent us boys out to the garage to get four of our corn knives and make sure they were good and sharp. Aunt Esther had arranged with three of the neighbor ladies to come and help make lunch and dinner for the silo filling hands. During the last week, Dad had contacted twelve of our neighbors with silos to help with silo filling. They were supposed to meet us at the cornfield before six-thirty that morning.

Virgil got behind the steering wheel of our 1935 Chevrolet and said, "Let's get going."

I put the jug of water and corn knives in the back and climbed in. Dad got in the front seat and we were off to the cornfield. We arrived to see two hundred rows of corn a quarter of a mile long with bright green corn leaves softly waving in the gentle morning breeze. Each stalk of corn had partially matured ears of corn, just right for cutting to fill the silo. Most of the help was already there. Our neighbors helping us were Elwin Bossomworth, Nelson Stine, Henry Swarms, Louie Fellers, Sam Fristoe, Roy Smith, Willard Ragel, Gerald Stine, Forest Anderson, Gus Durham, Howard Stine, Harry Bossomworth, and John Stine. We were all cutting corn to start with. Harry Bossomworth, Gerald Stine, Sam Fristoe, and Roy Smith came with their hay frame wagons and horses to help haul the corn from the field to the silage cutter at the silo.

If you are right handed, you use the corn knife with your right hand and cut the corn stalk off about two inches from the ground. You hold the stalk with your left hand, and as you cut more stalks let them lay back and rest against your left arm and elbow. When you get to the first pile of corn in your row, you put all you have cut on top of it. There are four rows in each pile. Whoever is in the lead going through the field determines how far apart the piles will be. It is usually a race to see who can get to the far end first. Once you start on a row you never look up, just keep cutting as fast as you can. When you get to the end of your row, you raise up, straighten out your back, wipe off the sweat, take a few deep breaths, and on your way back take the first row that is still standing. There were sixteen of us cutting corn, so if you were first to start back you take the seventeenth row, and go back to the end where we started. Usually six or eight start out together to see who can get to the far end first. My brother Virgil and Elwin Bossomworth ran a close race to see who could be first. As we got back to this end, we wiped the sweat, stretched to get the kinks out of our back, took a few deep breaths, and because we were now at the end, we also got a drink of that good cool well water. Then we continued this same routine, always getting a drink of water when we got back to the end where we started.

There was a creek that ran along the end of the cornfield and by the third time we got back to the starting end of the field, we were getting a little tired and hot. That old sun was quite high in the sky at mid-morning. We all laid down in the grass by the creek. My Dad, who was 55 years old and weighed about 200 pounds just rolled over about twice, right into the creek. He came up spitting water and declared that was a good way to cool off. But no one else tried it.

About that time, one of the cooks drove up with our midmorning lunch, some good cold ice tea and ice-cold lemonade. When Dad saw that, he got out of the creek and shook the water off so he could enjoy his lunch. After we finished our lunch and tanked up on ice-cold tea and lemonade, we returned to work. If we were going to get that silo filled, we needed to get some of the corn loaded on the wagons. Gerald and Sam liked to load up first. Four others pitched the bundles of corn up to them. That left the two champion corn cutters, Virgil and Elwin, plus eight more of us to go back to cutting corn. The race went on to see who could get to the other end first. When I got to the end of the row, wiped the sweat off, and got the kinks out of my back, Dad sent me to ride in with Gerald and Nelson so I could hitch the mules to the hay frame wagon and start hauling corn.

When we got home, Uncle Sterl had his International 15-30 tractor and the silage cutter in place. The silage cutter is driven by an endless belt from the tractor. The silage looks like mincemeat when it comes out of there. You need to keep your hands as far from the cutter as you can, the knife and blower are inside of a big drum. If you get too close while feeding the corn fodder in, it can be disastrous.

The blower can blow the silage up to the top of a sixty-foot silo. Our silo is very different from any of the other silos. We could not afford one of those big tall silos so we dug one in the ground, with a slip scraper and a team of horses. It was about twelve feet wide and eight to ten feet deep, with three vertical walls and the end near the barn was sloped so we could carry the silage out to feed the cows.

I hitched the team of mules up to the hay frame wagon and went back to the cornfield. John and Howard Stine were there to pitch the corn up on my wagon, I picked it up and stacked it crosswise on the wagon, starting in the back and piled it up as high as I could reach. This was a rather backbreaking job, because an armload of that green corn is quite heavy, especially for a scrawny 15-year-old kid. But I hauled as big of a load as anyone else. When John handed up the last pile of corn fodder in that row, he said that was about all we could haul on this load. I picked up the lines and headed the mules and wagon for home. As soon as I pulled up in the barnyard, I went to the well for a cup of that cold well water. It sure tasted good.

When Uncle Sterl called out for the next wagon, I pulled up to the end of that feeder trough. Uncle Sterl and Henry Swarms were on each side of the trough helping feed the corn stalks into that silage cutter. We kept that thing running at full capacity. Every few minutes I would drive the mules up just enough so that the corn, piled up on the wagon, would be even with the trough and keep feeding the corn in as fast as the silage cutter could take it. It was not long until I had the wagon unloaded and headed back out to the field for another load.

Willard Ragel and Forest Anderson pitched the corn up on my wagon this time. I stacked it crosswise with the butt end of the stalk to the right side of the wagon, so it would slide off into the silage feeder. I stacked another big load of green heavy bunches of corn as high as I could stack it. I got a little rest as the mules are pulling this load of corn back home and I was riding along on top of the load taking life easy. As I pulled in the driveway they were waiting for me, I pulled right up to the silage cutter and unloaded just like before.

Dad and everyone out in the field had come home and were eating dinner. I drove the mules back into the barnyard, unhitched, watered, and fed. When I got up to the house, the first group was through eating, and the second group was getting ready for dinner. We all washed up and enjoyed one of those delicious meals the ladies always fix at threshing and silo filling times.

After dinner, we were back to the same routine. Some were helping load the wagons, others were helping tromp or pack the silage in the silo. Dad asked Virgil to take over my wagon so I could put a saddle on Beauty, our riding horse, and ride her around in the silo to help pack the silage down. That sounded good to me. It was like getting a rest from cutting and hauling corn.

The silage in a trench silo needs to be packed down more than on the upright silo because with an upright the weight of 40 to 60 feet of silage help pack it. In a trench silo, you need several people and a horse to help pack it down.

We continued until we had all twenty acres of corn in that silo. When we finished we put about one foot of straw completely over the top and then covered that with about eight inches of dirt. That is the way you fill the silo when you have a trench silo.

INSTALLING NEW PISTON IN F-20 TRACTOR

It was June 23, 1937. I was cultivating corn on the Clint Dunbar farm, just west of St. James. I drove the tractor home for dinner today and as I pulled in the driveway and stopped in the shade of a tree, Dad came out on the back porch and hollered for me to drain the engine oil out of the tractor, before I came in to eat. We hadn't changed the oil since we started farming in the spring. I went out to the well and pumped several gallons of water in the cow and horse-watering trough so the water would be nice and cool. I drank a couple of cups full of that cool water, out of a rusty tin cup that hung on the pump. That is the best tasting water I ever drank.

I went and got a bucket and wrench to drain the oil. That oil sure is hot when it comes out of the engine. I got a rag out of the garage to wipe that hot oil off my hands then washed with soap and water on the back porch before going in the house for dinner. Dad had hired a housekeeper so we were eating pretty well now. Dad was a good cook, but when he worked in the field all day he didn't have much time to prepare meals. After dinner,

Dad and I went into the front room and sat down for a while to let our dinner settle. Dad had been cultivating corn with the mules over on the Henry Lowery farm and he thought the mules needed a few minutes more to rest also.

About ten minutes later, Dad said, "I guess you better put the oil back in the tractor and get back to cultivating that corn."

"Yeah, I was kind of thinking the same thing."

I picked up my straw hat, went out to the tractor, and picked up the drain plug and wrench. As I went to put the plug in the drain hole, I saw a big rounded piece of metal. It looked like the bottom skirt of a piston. I went back in the house and asked Dad to take a look at it.

"I think you are right. It sure looks like the skirt of the piston to me," he said.

The only thing to do was to get the wrenches and take the oil pan off. I went and got the ratchet, extension, and a couple of sockets. I loosened all of the pan bolts, then removed them and put them in a tin can. I took hold of the pan with one hand on each side near the bottom and applied pressure, first one side then the other. Almost immediately, it popped loose. I sat it off to one side, looked up into the engine and sure enough the entire skirt was broken off of the number three piston.

Dad had gone back in the house, waiting to hear the bad news. I went up on the porch and asked, "Dad do you want to come take a look at this thing? I don't know what happened, but the skirt is broken off the number three piston."

He came out, looked up inside, and said, "What do you think caused that?"

"I don't know. All I have done is drive this thing all day and half of the night, six days a week," I said.

Dad's question was could we get that piston out of the engine. Was there was enough room to take that rod and piston out through the bottom of the engine? Did we have a socket or wrench to fit those rod bolt nuts? I was quite sure I could do it. He helped me crank the engine over until the number three connecting rod was all the way down at the bottom, so I could work on it. Dad went in to call the International tractor dealer in St. Peter to see if they had a new piston to fit the tractor. I finally found a socket to fit the rod bolt nuts, and a two-foot length of pipe that would fit over the ratchet handle, so I could apply enough pressure to break the nuts loose. It was not too long until I had both nuts off and pushed the connecting rod up enough to clear the crankshaft, then put the connecting rod cap in the oil pan to keep it up out of the dirt. Dad came out of the house about that time. He said they had a piston with rings to fit the tractor. I asked him to crank the engine over maybe a quarter turn, so the piston would clear to come down out of there. He had to turn it real slow so I could pull the piston down to where it would clear the crankshaft. Dad started turning the crank and I pulled the rod and piston down part way.

I don't know [what caused the piston to break]. All I have done is drive this thing all day and half of the night, six days a week.

"Stop right there! I think the piston will clear the crank," I said. I pulled it down farther and sure enough, it came all the way out. I was quite excited about that. I think Dad was also. He didn't have to pay to get the engine overhauled and with luck I could be back to cultivating tomorrow. I handed Dad the piston and rod and said, "Have them put the new piston on the rod, because we don't have the tools to remove and replace the piston on the rod. I will clean the sludge out of the bottom of the oil pan, and I might take ten winks before you get back."

When Dad got back, I was in the front room asleep on the floor. I needed some rest as I had been driving the tractor many nights until ten o'clock or midnight, sometimes until one or two in the morning just to finish a job.

I spaced the gap on the compression rings 120 degrees from each other and the oil ring gap so it was not lined up with the bottom compression ring. Then I oiled the cylinder wall the best I could and oiled the piston and rod bearings and the crankshaft throw for the number three rod. I started the piston into the cylinder base up to the top compression ring. Then I put the ends of my fingers on the top compression ring opposite from the gap in the piston ring, pushed the ring in as far as I could, pushing up on the skirt of the piston, until the top compression ring was up inside of the cylinder. I did the same thing with the rest of the rings, including the oil ring, and then I pushed the rod and piston up into the cylinder far enough to place the connecting rod into the number three crankshaft throw.

Dale and brother on Farmall Tractor. Undated photo.

Then I put the rod-bearing cap onto the connecting rod, installed both nuts, and tightened them just a little tighter than they were when I removed them. I went to the garage, picked up the 5-gallon can of 40-weight motor oil and funnel, and checked the funnel to see if it was clean. I poured in what I thought was one and a half gallons of motor oil, then I checked it. It needed another quart. I poured in what I thought was a quart, let it set for a couple minutes, and checked it again. It looked good to me. I put the drain plug in and tightened it good. Don't forget that! I got out from under the tractor and cranked it over a couple of times. It felt just like it always did. I crawled out from under the tractor, straightened out my back, and went out to the well to get a drink of that good cool water from the rusty tin cup. Now, I was really proud of myself. I put a new piston in the tractor engine all by myself.

Dad came out and said, "I see you're putting oil in the tractor, so I guess you are all done."

"Yeah, I am all ready to start cultivating again."

We hoped to finish the corn on the Dunbar place before the day was out. It would take me until eight or nine o'clock. Dad said they would save dinner for me. As I fired it up and hit the throttle several times, it sounded just like new.

I WRECKED OUR 1935 CHEVROLET

"Dad, may I use the car to go down to the creek where we were swimming this afternoon. I forgot my water wings there and I need to go get them."

Dad said it was over two miles down there, a long way to drive just to get my water wings. I was just learning to swim and I really needed them. Dad finally let me take the keys hanging in the kitchen and had me take Forest along. Forest was my friend that had been swimming with us all afternoon. I thanked him, got the keys and just as I was getting in the car, Dad cautioned me to drive very carefully. As I started the car, I promised to be very careful. Forest got in the passenger side and we drove away very slow and carefully. It was a lot of fun getting to drive the car. I was real proud of myself. We went through St. James, and over the railroad track. Then I mashed down on the gas pedal and we were really flying. I never let off the gas until we were almost to the crossroad. Then I let off the gas, slammed my foot down on the brakes. That locked up all four wheels on the gravel road and skidded off to the left. I turned the steering wheel to the right. The car rolled over and landed on all four wheels in the ditch.

Forest was thrown out of the car through the left rear window. His neck was cut and he was bleeding badly. I was not hurt, just scared to death. I did not know what to do. Clint Dunbar lived about two hundred yards up the road. When he heard all the noise he and his son came down to see what happened. They tried to get the bleeding stopped, but we couldn't put a tourniquet on his neck, so they tried to stop the bleeding with hard pressure. Clint told his son, Peewee, to go home and tell his Mother to get some towels and come back in the car, because they needed to take Forest to the doctor in St. Elmo right now. I really felt bad about the whole thing but it was too late to do anything about it now. I told Clint I was sorry all of this happened, but I sure thanked him for helping Forest.

Clint's wife Mattie was there almost immediately. When she saw Forest, she said we needed to get to a doctor now. Clint and Forest got in the back seat. Clint was still trying to stop the bleeding. Mattie got in the front. I thanked them both very much for helping. I was still very nervous and scared.

After they left I looked the car over to see how badly it was wrecked, the left rear window that Forest went through was broken. The driver's door wind wing had been open and it was broken off. There was a small dent, hardly noticeable, on the rounded part of the roof just above the driver's door. I got in the car. It started right up so I pulled out of the ditch and drove home. I really did not want to go home, but there was nothing I could do about it now. I drove in the driveway, parked in front of the garage, got out, and looked the car over again. There didn't seem to be anything else wrong with it. I guess I was just stalling. I went into the house where Dad was in the living room reading the paper.

He looked up and asked me, "Did you get your water wings?"

"Well, no. As I was coming up to that state aid crossroad, I put on the brakes to slow down a little to see if any cars were coming, on that gravel road I guess the wheels skidded a little and I ended up in the ditch."

"You ended up in the ditch?" Dad got up out of his chair and looked around. "Where is Forest?" he asked.

I told him that Clint and Mattie Dunbar took him to the doctor.

"Why in the world did they take him to the doctor," Dad exclaimed.

"Well, when he went out through the rear window on the driver's side, he got his neck cut pretty bad. So Clint was trying to stop the bleeding and Mattie drove the car."

Now Dad was really excited. "How in the name of creation could Forest go out through the left rear window, when he was setting in the right front passenger seat?"

"Well! I… I don't… don't really… I don't really know Dad, but I think the car rolled over once before it landed in the ditch."

"Rolled over," Dad exclaimed, as he ran out the door to see the car.

I explained that all I could find wrong with the car was two broken windows and a little scrape here on the roof. Dad could hardly believe it rolled over and onto the wheels again with only two windows broken and a scrape above the door.

"You must have been doing ninety miles an hour, and I just let you drive the car to go get your water wings. I knew I shouldn't have let you drive the car in the first place," he said.

Since it was about milking time, Dad said, "Dale, why don't you go bring the cows in and milk them. See if you can do that the way your drive the car!"

Footnote: If any teenagers read this, do not drive the way I did. Drive the way my Dad told me to drive. Drive carefully – always.

TRADED THE 1935 CHEVY FOR A NEW CAR

It was a rainy day in March 1939, and we had just finished breakfast when Dad said we were going to take the 35 Chevy to St. Elmo to see if they would take it on trade for a new 1939 Chevy.

Virgil, being the main car driver of us boys, spoke up saying, "That thing runs horrible, I don't know if it will make it to St. Elmo or not."

It was only five miles to St. Elmo, and Dad said we needed to take it to a car dealer somewhere to trade it in. Virgil scurried out to the garage to get an extra can of oil because we would need it if we went farther than St. Elmo. It seemed to me like they were really going to trade cars today. I asked Dad if I could go. I was really interested in cars.

"Yes, but when I am trying to discuss the trade, you will be asking a thousand questions."

"No, Dad, I will be quiet," I promised.

"Well if you did, it would be the first time." Dad said okay, but warned me to be on my best behavior.

"You know I will be good," I said, as I jumped in the back seat.

Virgil came over, put the can of oil on the floor in the back seat, and got in the driver's seat. Dad got in the passenger side and shut the door as Virgil started the car and took off out of the driveway. Whoopee! We were off to get a new car. I was excited about that.

Virgil drove the half mile to St. James and stopped in front of the gas pump at the general store. I asked to pump the gas up into the glass tank. Virgil said for me to pump it up to the 10-gallon mark. There is a pump handle, about three feet long, that is pivoted at the bottom of the metal gas pump. As you pump this handle back and forth, it pumps the gas up into the glass tank on top, which has marks with the number at every gallon, up to 10 gallons. The tank needs to be up high because gravity moved the gasoline from the tank through a hose into your car's gas tank. As Virgil was putting the 10 gallons of gas in our car, Dad went into the store and paid Bill Miller, the storeowner, for the gas. Gas was 10 cents a gallon, so it cost $1 for the 10 gallons.

Virgil got in and we were on our way to St. Elmo to trade for a new Chevy. I was quite excited as Virgil pulled up in front of Phillip Chevrolet Garage and said, "Well, we made it this far."

We all got out of the car and made a run to get into the garage, out of the rain. We went into the show room looking at the new cars. Mr. Phillips came over and started talking to Dad, and then we went out into the garage to look at more cars that were new. Mr. Phillips showed Dad a dark green 4-door sedan. Dad seemed quite interested in it so Mr. Phillips said he needed to drive our car if we wanted to trade it in. Dad said that was no problem and pointed out that we were parked right in front of the garage, pointing to our black '35 Chevy. The rain had slacked up, so we all went out to the car. Mr. Phillips got in to drive and Dad sat up front with him. Virgil and I got in the back. Mr. Phillips started the engine. It put out a cloud of blue smoke from the exhaust.

He said, "I don't think you have this thing trained to quit smoking yet have you?"

Dad answered, "Yeah, it smokes a little when you first start it up."

Mr. Phillips went south on Main Street out to the highway, stepped on the gas pretty hard, and got it up to about 50 mph and another cloud of smoke. Mr. Phillips remarked, "This thing doesn't have enough power to get out on the highway, but it isn't short on blue smoke."

Dad replied it was not a new car.

"Well, there is no way I could sell this car, so I can't even take it in on a trade," Mr. Phillips replied.

Dad said we would take it to Burtchi's Garage in Vandalia, and maybe he would give us something for it on a trade. Mr. Phillips quickly said he could sell Dad a new car for the same price or maybe cheaper than Burtchi. Dad said no, that we would go over there and see what they could do. With that, Virgil got back in the driver's seat and we were on our way to Vandalia. When we arrived at Burtchi's Chevrolet Garage, Virgil parked on the side street west of the garage and put a couple of quarts of oil in.

Dad said, "With it parked over here maybe he won't want to drive it."

Virgil put oil in the car, and then we all went into the garage show room with a couple of new 1939 Chevys in it. It wasn't long until a salesman came out and started talking to Dad. Virgil and I were raising the hood and checking the engine, checking out the driver's seat, and looking it over. As I got out of the car, I heard Dad say to the salesman that we had a 1935 Chevrolet as a trade in on that car. The man asked where it was parked; he needed to see it. Dad told him it was over there on the west side of the garage.

The salesman said, "Well, let's go take a look at it. I need to take it on a short drive."

Virgil and I walked out after them. I was careful not to say anything. I did not want to interrupt them or get into trouble. When we got out to the car Virgil gave the keys to the salesman and we all got in.

As he backed out into the street, he backed right through a cloud of blue smoke and remarked, "This thing sure is a smoker."

Dad acknowledged that it did smoke a little when you first start it.

Vandalia is right on the Kaskaskai River so there are quite a few hills on most streets. The salesman had to shift down into second on about every hill. He noted that the car sure didn't have much power as he drove it back to the garage. Dad asked him what he would allow on a trade for the 4-door green car in the show room. He said he couldn't allow anything because he wouldn't be able to sell our car. However, he would be glad to sell that green car today. Dad said he wasn't interested unless the salesman would allow $100. for the '35 Chevy.

"Not interested," he said as he walked back into the garage.

Virgil got back in the driver's seat and asked, "Where do we go now?"

Dad directed Virgil to go east there on Main Street a block or two, and take that new Route 51 North.

"It is only about 15 miles up to Ramsey and they have a Chevrolet garage," he said.

That old Chevy smoked all the way to Ramsey. The Chevrolet garage there was a very small garage compared to the Chevy garage in Vandalia, but they had new Chevrolets there including 4-door sedans.

The salesman came out and began telling Dad all about the new inventions on these cars; the steering column and the transmission shift lever with vacuum boost. Dad told the salesman the only accessory he wanted on the car was a heater. The salesman said he had a green 4-door sedan with a heater right there in the showroom. They went over and looked it over. Dad said it was what he wanted and that he had a 1935 Chevy to trade in. The man said that was okay, he would take it for a drive and maybe we could make a deal. I thought to myself that it was doubtful.

As we walked out to the car, the salesman turned around and asked Virgil and I if we drove the car much? Virgil answered that he drove quite a bit. I kept quiet. I don't think I drove any after I wrecked it in July 1937.

After driving a short distance on route 51 the salesman pointed out, "This car don't seem to have much power and puts out quite a lot of smoke."

As we were on the way back to the garage Dad asked what the salesman would give as a trade in for the 4-door sedan we looked at.

"I don't think I could sell your car if I took it in on a trade. But if you buy it today I will allow you $50 for it."

"Fifty," Dad exclaimed. "I was thinking more like $150."

The salesman said he was taking a chance at $50, but thought if Dad wanted to buy the new car, he might be able to get a partial loan at the local bank. As we pulled up in front of the garage, Dad said he wasn't interested and that he needed to get over $100 for the 35 Chevy. The salesman got out of the car and offered again to sell Dad the 4-door sedan.

"Not today," Dad said.

Virgil got back into the driver's seat and said, "What now?"

Dad said we would stop by the Chevrolet garage in Altamont. Altamont was 45 or 50 miles away. Virgil asked me to give him the can of oil. He poured the oil in and said there was about one quart of oil left in the can. If we didn't get rid of the car soon we would have to buy more oil. Virgil got in and we were on our way to Altamont.

As we were driving along I said, "Dad, I sure hope we can get a new car in Altamont. This car won't go 50 mph, and it drinks oil like a camel drinks water in the desert."

Dad said, "If they offer me anything for this car I am going to buy the new car."

It wasn't long until we were in the Chevrolet Garage in Altamont. We went through the same procedure there. When the salesman showed Dad the green 4-door sedan, Dad said he had a 1935 Chevrolet for a trade in. The salesman responded that he needed to drive it first. He drove it there in Altamont, out on the route a short distance, and pointed out that it smoked a lot and seemed to be down on power.

Then he asked, "What do you want for it?"

Dad replied, "I need $100 to make a trade."

The salesman thought about that as he was running numbers through his head, then he said, "I can give you $80 and that is it."

Dad thought about it for a while and then he said, "I won't let $20 stand between me and a new car. I'll take it."

Virgil and I jumped up and down. We got a new Chevy! We went over to check it out, checked the paint, all of the seats, the engine, we even checked out the trunk. We were really excited about our new car. After Dad signed all of the papers, the car was ours, but we did owe some money on it yet.

Dad asked if we liked the new car and we cried in unison, "Oh, yes!"

Dad drove the new car home and said how glad he was that we got rid of the '35 Chevy. It had burned 10 gallons of gas and 2 quarts of oil in less than 100 miles. As we drove home, Dad sure liked the feel of the new car. We all enjoyed our new 1939 Chevy until it was wrecked in less than a year.

FAYETTE COUNTY FAIR

It was July 1939. The Fayette County Fair meant, Ferris Wheels, Merry-Go-Rounds, circular swings, and the Midway, with all kinds of games, throwing baseballs at bottles, pitching coins in a container, food booths of all kinds, and cotton candy. Anything to entertain the crowd. To me, it meant something entirely different this year. My three older brothers had all gone somewhere else to work. I was the youngest in the family, but now it was my turn for the job to take care of the livestock at the fair. We took a team of mules, the largest mules in Fayette County, a herd of Holstein cows, which consisted of a bull, one mild cow, a heifer, and a calf, a pen of Poland China pigs, which were a boar, one sow, and one shoat. The livestock listed is what Dad took the first time he went to the fair back in 1933. The prize money was very good. He made more money at the fair than he did farming all year. Corn was only ten cents a bushel. When he shipped hogs to the market, what he got paid, sometimes wouldn't even pay the freight bill to send them to the market. Dad bought some registered Ayrshire cattle, raised his own herd of cattle to take to the fair, and sold some. He also bought registered Ohio Improved Chester White hogs just to take to the fair and, also for sale. He also bought a ram sheep and some ewes and raised his own flock of sheep.

This year I was there taking care of the livestock for seven days and nights. I had the team of mules, the herd of Holstein cows, Ayrshire cows, Poland China hogs, Ohio Improved Chester White hogs, and the flock of sheep. You need to feed and water everything twice a day, clean out the stalls, and put fresh straw in their pens twice a day, and milk the cows every morning and evening. I drank some of the milk, but I also took some down to the Midway about nine o'clock in the morning. I sold some of the milk, about 50 cents to a dollar's worth, which was enough for a ride on the Ferris Wheel. Not too bad. I could have been out there barefooted, shocking wheat in the hot sun for dinner and a dollar a day.

On the day the animals were judged, we gave them a bath, curried and brushed them, and brushed out the tails on the mules and the cows to make them look good. If they got first place, or maybe champion, the prize money was higher. In fact, the Holstein bull got first place, champion, and grand champion, the last four years. He was our best moneymaker. So we put up with him being a little cantankerous at times. Dad was always there early on any of the days that some of the livestock was to be judged. He wanted to be sure they looked their best and knew exactly how they should stand to look their best when being judged.

When the judging was all over, we got our entry book and the ribbons in each category and we should have had $680 coming. But after Dad got the Ayrshire cows, Ohio Improved Chester White hogs, and the sheep, that was about what we had made every year for the last four years. Dad and I were both quite excited about that, as this is more money than we ever made farming in any one year. Because $680 was a lot of money in the Nineteen

Thirties. Needless to say, we were both quite proud of that.

Footnote: Ralph Waldo was from Alton, Illinois. Alton is about 65 miles southwest of Brownstown, Illinois, which is the location of the Fayette County Fair. Ralph Waldo is in the Guinness's book of records for the world's tallest man. He was there at the fair one day that year. He was 8 feet tall and wore size 36 shoes. He drove up in a Plymouth sedan. He took the front seat out, and sat in the back seat to drive the car.

HYDRAULIC BRAKES ON HAROLD'S PICKUP

Harold Lash came by the house one morning, on his milk route to pick up our two ten-gallon cans of milk. He asked me to go to Shelbyville with him later that day to take the hydraulic brake system off a 1939 pickup. I told him I would be glad to. He planned to go home and get his tools after he finished the milk deliveries, then he would come back by to pick me up about two hours later.

It was a cold, rainy day in March 1940, mostly just a drizzle. It was too wet to work in the field. Besides, I would rather work on that truck than follow a walking plow all day.

Harold Lash was a good friend of mine. He was also a good mechanic. He drove a 1937 Ford pickup truck on this milk route, picking up milk in ten-gallon cans from the farms in the area. He would then deliver it to the dairy in Altamont, about 12 miles from our house. The load of milk and milk cans is about one to one-and-a-half-ton, on his half-ton truck. The problem on his 1937 Ford pickup is the cable-actuated brakes. The sand from the gravel roads tends to stick on the exposed section of the cable and every time you apply the brakes it pulls the sand back into the cable shield. After driving this route 365 days a year for about three years, it is almost impossible to apply the brakes.

About ten-thirty, Harold pulled in the driveway and I went out and hopped into the truck. Harold said, "Are you ready to pull the brakes of that truck?"

"Sure. It sounds interesting to me. Besides, I will learn a lot about cars working with you," I replied.

Harold was anxious to get some brakes on the truck, so he could come to a stop with a full load of milk.

"It is almost impossible to stop this thing now," he complained.

In no time, we had driven the 30 miles to Shelbyville. Harold had directions to the wrecking yard. We stopped by the office and Harold went in to tell the owner he was looking for a brake system from the 1939 Ford pickup they had talked about on the phone. Harold told me they wanted $20 for the entire brake system because it was practically a new truck. The owner already had it up on stands, just at the end of the building. We drove straight down between the two rows of wrecked cars to a blue pickup almost to the far end on the right side. As we drove down there, Harold said he was glad to pay $20 to have a truck that would stop.

I was really excited we were going to take the brake system off of the 1939 Ford to make Harold's truck safe to drive. As we got out, Harold had me go and push down on the brake pedal to see if it all worked, then hold it down and he loosened the lug nuts. We had to take off the wheels to get to the brakes. I got in the truck from the passenger door, as the other side was really smashed. I pushed down on the brake pedal, and told Harold that the brakes seemed okay. He loosened all the lug nuts while I held the brake pedal down so the wheels wouldn't turn. We took all four of the wheels and the brake drums off. The brake linings looked like new. We then disconnected the brake lines from all four wheel cylinders and let the brake fluid run out on the ground. Next, we unbolted the rear brake backing plates, from the rear axle housing, and unbolted the front brake plates from the front spindles. The brake plates have the wheel cylinder, the brake adjuster, the brake shoes, and all of the mechanism to actuate the brake shoes, attached to the plates. Next, we unfastened all of the brake lines and fittings from the body and chassis of the truck. We removed them, trying to keep the steel brake lines in the same bent condition they were originally installed in, the best we could, and still get them out of the truck.

We were now ready to remove the brake and clutch pedals from the inside of the vehicle, also the brake master cylinder, actuation rod, and brake fluid reservoir. After we got this all removed, we put a tag on each backing plate to indicate which wheel position it was removed from and loaded everything in the truck. Once we had it all loaded we searched diligently in and around the pickup to be sure we had every part including nuts, bolts and brackets, we needed to install a complete hydraulic brake system on the 1937 Ford pickup.

Harold was satisfied that we had every part that we needed. He went in to pay for it and we headed for home. On the way home, Harold asked me to help me install this brake system the next day. I had thought we would start as soon as we got home. However, Harold said he hadn't planned on doing the milk route tomorrow with the horses and wagon. He wanted to start early tomorrow to be sure we get the job completed. Harold dropped me off at home and told me to be ready and he would pick me up after his route in the morning.

"You know I will be ready. I am probably more excited about this than you are. This may be the only 1937 Ford pickup in the country that has hydraulic brakes, and you and I are the ones that did it."

Sure enough, he pulled in about ten-thirty the next morning. I ran out and jumped in. Harold said, "Are you ready to tackle this job?"

I was ready. I had been excited about this ever since he first mentioned doing it. Harold pulled into the garage. We got out of the truck and got started. He loosened all of the lug nuts on all four wheels, and then he asked me to get the four jack stands and put them under the frame on each end, after he jacked the truck up. We shook the truck to be sure it was safe to work on.

Harold said, "We are going to take the brake system off of this truck just like we did on that 1939 truck at the wrecking yard, only now we are removing cables, cable housing, and the actuating arm."

We had to remove the clutch and brake pedals from inside of the truck cab. When we finished that, Harold suggested we take a break and see if Helen, Harold's wife, would fix us something for lunch. He then hollered at his son, Sonny, to come get something to eat. Sonny was helping us, sometimes carrying around the tool we were looking for or trying to help us with the tool he happened to have in his hand. Sonny was pushing two years old but he got about as greasy as we did. We all washed up for lunch.

As we went in the kitchen Helen said, "I thought you were never coming in for lunch. I have some hot soup and a sandwich for you."

That hot soup sure sounded good, as it was a rather cool damp day in March.

As we were eating lunch, Helen asked how things were going with the new brake system.

Harold answered, "We have all of that old junky brake system off of the '37 and are ready to install the best hydraulic brake system in the country for a 1937 pickup."

Actually, we were all excited to get the job finished so we could take it out on the road and test it. Immediately after lunch, we were back in the garage. We put the brake backing plates on first and made sure to get them on the correct side of the truck, or the brake shoes would be on backwards. We installed all of the metal tubing and flex hoses, fastening them to the frame and rear axle as they were on the 1939 pickup. Then we installed the clutch and brake pedals, the brake master cylinder, and hydraulic reservoir. We had to drill holes in the firewall to mount the master cylinder and another hole for the brake push rod. The push rod, attached to the brake pedal, goes from the brake pedal, thru the firewall, into the master cylinder. So when you push on the brake pedal the master cylinder forces brake fluid out to all four-wheel cylinders. When the wheel cylinders extend, it applies the brakes to all four wheels equally. Harold had me go around and tighten all of the brake lines, nuts, and fittings. Harold reminded me not to attach the lines to the master cylinder because we needed to bleed all of the air out of it first.

Now that everything was installed we checked to see that all of the brake line, nuts and fittings were tight and checked all of the lines, to be sure they are not rubbing against the frame or body. After we finished that, Harold filled the brake reservoir with brake fluid. I held my fingers lightly over the master cylinder outlet fittings so the brake fluid would not leak out, but the air could escape, while Harold pumped the brake pedal slowly. After we got all of the air out, we connected the brake lines to the master cylinder and then installed all four brake drums in the same position they were in on the 1939 pickup.

Now we were ready to bleed the brakes to get all of the air out of the brake lines and wheel cylinders. Harold filled the brake reservoir and said he would bleed the brakes, while I pushed the brake pedal down and held it until he told me to release it.

We went through that cycle about five times, and then he said, "Fill the brake reservoir again."

We went through this procedure for all four wheel brake cylinders. I was really getting excited now! We were about ready to test these hydraulic brakes on this 1937 Ford pickup. Harold was excited too.

"Let's put the wheels on this thing and try it," he said.

We put the wheels on and tightened all of the lug nuts. Harold jacked up the truck while took out the jack stands. We could hardly wait to see how the brakes worked.

Harold got in the truck and started the engine. I got in the passenger side. He let it roll forward about two feet, pushed down the brake pedal and it stopped immediately. He turned on the headlights and drove out onto the road. Trying the brakes several times, as he drove down the road he got it up to about 40 miles an hour on a dirt road. He applied the brakes and it came to an immediate stop.

Harold said, "This is a piece of cake, nothing like those old cable brakes.

He turned around at the corner and asked me if I wanted to drive back.

"Sure! We put in a lot of work on this thing. I'd like to try it out."

We changed seats, and I tried the brakes a few times. Then speed up to about 40 miles per hour, and squeezed the brakes on firmly. It came to a quick stop.

I said, "This thing will stop on a dime with a nickel change. This is probably the only 1937 Ford in existence with hydraulic brakes."

GERMANY SURRENDERS

When Germany surrendered, it was the end of war in Europe. So there was no more demand for B-17 Bombers in Europe any longer. I was a B-17 engine mechanic and there was a big demand for C-54 engine mechanics in North Africa. The main supply line for personnel and supplies was the North Africa Division of the Air Transport Command. Their route from the United States to the war effort in China, Burma, India, and the Pacific was from Miami, Florida, to Natal, Brazil to Dapper, Africa, right on the equator, to Casablanca, to Maiketch, in North Africa, to Cairo, Egypt, then on to Karachi, India. If the weather was just right and the plane was not overloaded, they would fly from Casablanca, in North Africa, to the Canary Islands, then direct to Miami, Florida.

Now it wasn't but a couple of weeks after Germany surrendered that we packed our barracks bags and toolboxes and were on our way to Casablanca, French Morocco. We were paid one time in good old U. S. dollars and cents before we left England. But out next payday was French Francs and Centimes. As we were loading on to the B-17, I was the last one to go aboard. The fuselage section was jam packed so the loadmaster told me to go all the way forward to the bombardier section. I was quite happy about that as the seat is right in the Plexiglas nose section, and you have a good 270-degree view of everything ahead of you. Now this is a good 10-hour flight, so I was glad to have a reasonably comfortable seat. But as soon as I could see land, as we were cruising that section of the Atlantic Ocean, west of Gibraltar, I could see that we're exactly lined up with that runway of the Casablanca Airport. I kept my eyes right on that runway as we kept getting closer and closer. As we passed the end of the runway, the pilot sat the plane down so smooth. You could hardly tell when the wheels hit the runway.

Dale in Army uniform. Undated photo.

The pilot taxied over to the loading and unloading zones and as we unloaded the Sergeant there hollered, "Okay, you ground pounders, put your tool boxes over there by the building. You did put your name and serial number on your boxes didn't you?"

"Yeah," we all answered in unison.

"Now get your rear end and your barracks bag on one of these trucks and they will take you over to Camp Dushane for reassignment."

I asked the Sergeant, "When are we going to get something to eat?"

"They will feed you when you get over to Camp Dushane."

"Well, I sure hope so. We are all starving."

"Just hop up in the truck. You will survive."

He was right. We all did survive. They pulled the truck up in front of our barracks. The barracks was a tent about 80 feet long with a row of Army cots down each side. The Sergeant told us to go put our barracks bag on our bunk of choice and then dinner would be waiting for us at the mess hall.

The Sergeant said, "It is about 300 yards to the left, down this road just in front of the truck. You will smell it before you get there."

The Sergeant was right again. We all chowed down, wandered back to our tent, and checked out our surroundings. It was very hot in the tent in midafternoon. But this was much better than a fox hole half full of water and ice in the winter time.

In a replacement camp, there is not much to do. So we went down to the PX, had a cup of coffee, and a donut occasionally. We started talking to a group of African-American truck drivers that were stationed in Italy. Eventually the conversation got around to playing softball.

Richard Arbee, our catcher, spoke up. "We have a baseball team also. Maybe we could get together and play a game."

They were all excited about that.

Their spokesman replied, "We have been in Italy about three years and never lost a game."

"Well, we have only been playing about one and a half years, won two or three, and lost about the same. But if we can get our team together, we would sure enjoy a game with you all."

A couple of days after this conversation, several of us were down at the PX for our coffee and donuts. Sergeant Arbee was there. He asked one of the truck drivers from Italy, "Are you ready for a ball game today?"

"Sure, we are ready."

I suggested, "Let's meet down at the ball diamond about six o'clock today. It might be a little cooler then. We might even get a slight ocean breeze."

This was June in North Africa, so normally quite hot. We all met at the ball diamond about six o'clock. Now, our catcher and our pitcher were about 80 percent of the strength of our team. Our pitcher could really pitch that softball and Arbee, our catcher, kept those batters frustrated with his incessant jabbering.

I can still hear him saying, "Batter, batter, batter, look out. Here comes the fastball." And it would be a slow ball.

He sat up so close to the batter sometimes it looked he would grab that ball right out from in front of the bat. Arbee would holler, "Hey, you missed it again." Then he would show the batter the ball right in his catchers mit and say, "Here it is right here." He kept up this routine for every ball pitched for every batter.

The baseball diamond was all sand. There was no grass this time of year and it was very hot. But we finally won the game with a score of five to three.

AFRICA HIGHLIGHTS

On the first of June 1945, they called all of the personnel from Molesworth, England together. We were all separated out and assigned to the five different air bases across Africa, from Draku on the Enatae to Kouchi, India. I lucked out. Several other of the engine mechanics and I stayed right there in Casablanca.

Sometimes, two mechanics worked on an airplane and sometimes one mechanic worked alone. I was changing this engine all by myself. I had the engine completely installed, but if the change was due to engine failure, rather than maximum engine life, you also had to change the oil cooler. I had just removed the oil cooler, went to supply, and got a new cooler. Sarge hollered that it was dinnertime. I set the new cooler down by the right hand landing gear, as this was the number three engine that I was changing.

I went to dinner with the rest of the gang that was working in the hanger. The dinner was a typical Army Air Corp dinner, fried chicken wings (or sea gulls, I am not sure which) with mashed potatoes and chicken gravy, with a nice big peach half and thick peach juice served right in the middle of your mashed potatoes and gravy. We also had imitation grapefruit juice, which we called Battery Acid, served in a twenty gallon GI can.

When I got back to the hanger after dinner, I got my tools and the oil cooler, got up on the washstand, put the oil cooler in place, and secured the mounting strips. As I started to install the oil in-and-out lines, I saw the used engine oil on the cooler fittings and yelled, "Oh, my goodness," and a few other Army Air Corp learned expletives, "this is the old cooler. How in the world could I have made that mistake?"

Anyway, I went to work and removed the old oil cooler, and installed the new one. You only need to install new oil coolers and flush the oil lines when they have an engine failure with metal particles in the oil. If it is an engine change because the engine has reached maximum engine life of seven hundred fifty hours, you are not required to change the oil cooler.

After I finished the oil cooler installation, I checked everything on the engine, and installed the engine cowling. I went and got the tug driver to pull the plane out of the hanger, then hook on the front end and pull it out on the flight line. The C-54 has a small steering wheel down and forward to the left of the pilot's flight controls that you steer the airplane with. Then there is a painted green line, about fifteen inches wide on the floor of the hanger, that you keep the front wheels on to keep from hitting any of the hangers, or airplanes on the flight lines.

About the time we were past the hanger on my right, I heard a big explosion, as if a bomb had exploded. I was sure I had hit the hanger with the right wing. I was really scared.

The thought went through my mind, "I will have to stay in the Army another twenty years to pay for this stupid airplane."

I got down off the airplane expecting the worse. I didn't see any damage to the wing, but the airplane was sure leaning to the right. Then I saw that I had a flat tire. It was blown to shreds. I sure breathed a sigh of relief at that. As soon as I got my breath, I went out to the flight line and got the crew chief for the plane. I told him I had a flat on the plane that we had just changed the engine on.

Dale in Army uniform. Undated photo.

"Yeah, I know. We take off all of the good tires on planes that go into the hanger for major repairs and put on the tires that have the cord showing on the tread."

It's a good thing the pilot didn't try to make another landing with that tire! I headed back to get someone to help me change the wheel and tire.

When it was ready, I got the tug driver to pull the plane out to the flight line and I steered the plane to keep that front wheel right on the green line. After we got the plane in place on the flight line, the tug driver put the chocks in front and behind the wheels, then he stood by while I started the number three engine and checked the oil, fuel pressure and then checked both magnetos. Everything was okay except that I had to raise the oil pressure. I went and got a crew chief's stand and pushed it up to the right hand side of the engine. I went back and got the tools I needed to adjust the oil pressure, and then put them in a bucket of water. You have to put your tools in a bucket of water when working on the flight line in the summer time because they will get so hot you can't hold them. I set the bucket of tools up on the crew chiefs stand.

As soon as I shut the engine down, the oil truck pulled up and they started filling the number three engine oil tank. The filler cap is on the right hand side of the engine nacelle, just back of the firewall. I got up on the engine stand, got the tools I needed out of the bucket of water, stuck my head into the accessory section of the engine compartment and started adjusting the oil pressure. About the time I got the oil pressure adjusted, a stream of hot 1200 weight engine oil hit me right in the back of my head. The oil ran down into my face and down my back. I closed my eyes so the oil wouldn't get into my eyes.

The Sergeant filling the oil tank said, "I'm sorry. I am sorry. I just pulled the hose up a little to see if the tank was about full. The hose must have been twisted. It snapped out of the tank filler and the oil streamed out."

I told him I was okay, then took an oil rag out of my pocket, and wiped the oil off of my face and forehead. I went back into the hanger and washed down real good with 115-octane aviation gas. Then I went to the barracks and washed down good with soap and hot water, before someone smoking a cigarette set me on fire!

I went back out to the airplane and got someone to stand by while I started the engine again and check the oil pressure. This time it was okay. I secured and safety-wired the oil pressure adjusting screw. I got the engine cowling out of the hanger, installed it, and called it a day. It was chow time now anyway.

BUYING AN AUTOMOBILE IN SPAIN

September 1962, I took a job in Seville Spain, as a quality control representative for the U.S. Air Force at S.E.R.I.M.A., a Spanish aircraft company. They were overhauling F-102 aircraft for the Strategic Air Command.

My wife, four children, ranging in ages 11 through 19, and I all moved to Seville. Being a typical American born and raised in the United States, the land of the automobile, I felt I needed an automobile. There were no automobile dealers in Spain with a showroom full of cars. You bought your car from a car salesman who had a small cubicle about eighty square feet. He had brochures for cars made in England, Germany, France, and Italy. We narrowed the choice down to either the German Ford or the Italian Fiat. The Fiat won out. It was a six-cylinder car with more room than the Ford. We picked out the color we wanted, and paid him. It cost a little over $1,200.

He handed me the receipt and said, "The car should be up at Irun,

Dale Ragel family in Spain, 1962.

the free port entry, on the French boarder in three to four weeks. I will bring all of the paperwork you need to pick up your car to the Niza Hotel."

I told him I would probably be in to bug him three or four times before it arrived.

We finally found an apartment and moved in about November 20. I stopped by the car sales office to let him know we had moved. The car salesman said the car should be there any day. I sure hoped so. I was tired of walking and trying to find the right bus to where I needed to go. Sure enough, he came to our apartment the next evening with all of the paper work I needed to pick up the Fiat in Irun and my airline ticket to San Sebastian. I had to leave Seville at seven o'clock the next morning, November 23. I wanted to get an early start so I could get to Irun in time to get through customs and hopefully drive back to Madrid before dark.

Dick Story, the American I was riding to work with, picked me up about six-thirty a.m. He took me to the airport, which is where we both worked. I was on the airplane a little after seven o'clock and had a very uneventful flight to Madrid. We got there in about two hours and as soon as I got off the plane, I went to the Iberia airline counter and asked where to catch the flight to San Sebastian. He said it would leave from this gate right here at nine-thirty. In about 15 minutes, the announcement came over the loud speaker that the flight had been delayed until ten-thirty, so I went over and sat down to wait. I really wasn't relaxed, because I wanted to get to Irun in time to get my Fiat through customs that day.

The next announcement about the flight to San Sebastian said the flight had been delayed until eleven-thirty, then later that it was delayed until one o'clock p.m. I thought I could forget about getting through customs that day. I tried to relax a little, as I was not getting anywhere anyway. I went to the snack bar to get a sandwich and a bottle of gaseosa. Gaseosa is somewhat like the soft drink 7-Up after you get used to it. About the time I finished my lunch, news came over the sound system that the flight to San Sebastian had been cancelled. I thought to myself maybe Americans do not really need a car. I went over to the airline counter, there were about twenty irate people asking what to do now. The clerk explained that there would be a bus along in a few minutes to take us down to the train station. He would announce when it got there. There was a big snowstorm in northern Spain. The San Sebastian airport was closed and that is what was causing all the problems. In the crowd, I noticed some other Americans. You can tell them by the way they dress. I introduced myself and started talking to them. They were James, his wife Janet, and another man named Lloyd. They were in the Air Force at Torrejon Air Force Base near Madrid. They were also going to pick up two cars in Irun. We visited for a while waiting for the bus.

In about an hour, they announced the bus was there to take us to the train station and they would accept the airline tickets to San Sebastian. We all loaded on the bus and eventually made it to the train station. I took my airline ticket up to the cashier and asked him what time the train would leave for San Sebastian.

He answered, 'A las ocho," and something after that I didn't understand.

I asked, "A los ocho y media?"

"No! A las ocho en punto, en punto." This meant eight o'clock sharp.

Well, the train left about nine o'clock p.m. When I got on the train, the aisle was on one side of the car and the passenger compartments on the other side. There was a sliding door and seats fore and aft, facing each other. It also had glass on the aisle side of the compartment so you could see who was in the aisle and see out the window on that side. I was in the compartment with four or five other people, one of them a Catholic priest. He and a couple of the other passengers spoke some English. They were quite curious about what I was doing in Spain and where I was going. I told them I worked at the Seville Airport and was going to Irun to pick up my new Fiat. We discussed quite a lot about my work and the reason I was going to Irun to pick up my car. I explained that the main reason I was going to Irun was because it was a free port. If I bought a car made in a foreign country while I was in the United States I'd have to pay a 100% tax on it. But if I bought it out of the country and had all of the necessary legal papers, I could import it without paying the taxes. However, when I leave Spain I must take the car with me since I cannot sell it here.

I was beginning to get sleepy, as it was now about midnight. I went out in the aisle to go to the rest room. It was really cold out there. When I came back to my compartment, it was cold also, but nothing like out in the aisle. I curled up in the seat and pulled my overcoat up over me and in no time, I was asleep.

The next morning after daylight, I saw the three Americans from Madrid walk by the window so I went out and talked with them. From the looks of all the snow out there, we might have trouble driving back to Madrid. It looked like the white shiny stuff was a foot deep or more. We planned to all stick together, so we took a taxi from the train station over to the customs office. We also planned to drive back to Madrid together, in case we get stuck in this snow. That sure sounded good to me, however I did have a set of tire chains in my suitcase, which I would most likely need.

We were getting cold out in the aisle so I went back in the compartment where it was reasonably warm.

The train was very slow through the Pyrenees Mountains in northern Spain and the snow made the trip that much longer. However, we finally made it to San Sebastian a little after one o'clock p.m. When the train came to a stop in the train station, I breathed a sigh of relief. I was not sure if we would make it through all of the snow in the mountains. I said good-bye to the rest and "Adios" to the Spaniards and picked up my suitcase on the way out. I met up with the three Americans. Lloyd had been here before and led us to a taxi just outside the front door. We walked out and Lloyd went to talk to the driver. He looked back at us and told us to hop in. The driver was going to take us to Irun. We got in the taxi and were on our way to Irun, about twelve miles away. There were ruts and chuckholes in the snow, which was frozen, and made driving very difficult. It took over an hour to get there. We were all overjoyed to make it to the customs office finally. We each paid the taxi driver a third of the fare plus tip, and he was on his way. I was not sure what surprises awaited us at the customs office.

We all had our paperwork ready and laid it on the counter. The customs officer looked at us very surprised and asked if all three of us were picking up a car. I told him that was what we were here for. He took us one at a time to make sure all of the necessary paperwork was in order. The salesmen that sell these cars from a brochure must know exactly what is required to get through customs, because we all went through without any

Our first Fiat. Ready to go camping. Undated photo.

problems. He gave all of us a license plate and all of the necessary registration papers for our cars. He then took us out back, pointed out our cars and wished us luck getting back to Madrid with all of the snow.

The roads were a mess and he thought that the only roads that would still be open went through Pamplona and then to Zaragoza, then back to Madrid. We thanked him and headed to our cars. Janet spoke up asking if we could get something to eat now that we finally had our cars. I knew everybody was starving, but if we could make it through most of the mountains before dark, it might be a lot quicker and safer. I don't think Janet was too happy but her husband James, agreed. He said the roads were not numbered and if we get out there and get lost in the mountains with all of this snow, it might take several days to get back to Madrid. It seemed like the logical thing to do was to head out for Pamplona.

Lloyd had been here before, so I suggested he take the lead to Pamplona. Lloyd agreed saying he would do the best he could leading us back toward San Sebastian. So we all headed out for the mountains and the snow in our new cars. We only got about 15 kilometers out of town and there was a big truck stopped off to the left side of the road on a very steep hill. We stopped because the road was sloped sharply to the right, right over the side into the canyon.

The truck driver came over and said it was too steep. He couldn't make it up the hill in the snow. I think the most dangerous thing was if the wheels start spinning the cars could easily slide right over the side into the canyon. So we all stood around for a while discussing what we should do. We finally decided two of us would push from the side of the car to keep it from sliding into the canyon and two would help push from the back, up the hill. I cautioned the driver not to give it too much gas, which might cause the wheels to spin.

We decided James should try it first, as the Volkswagen had the engine in the rear with much more weight on the driving wheels. James agreed but said to make sure not to let him and the car slide down into the canyon. Janet just stood over to the side shaking her head. She was sure we were all crazy. She might be right, but what else could we do.

James got in the car, we got behind and to the right side of the car, and pushed. James drove it right up the hill. We pushed until he got past the most dangerous spot. He drove on for about an eighth of a mile where the road leveled off a little and the canyon wasn't right at the roadside. He parked there and walked back to help the next car up.

In the meantime, I got my tire chains out of my suitcase so I could get up the hill by myself. When James got back, I told Lloyd to go up next, and then the two of them could go on. I would put the chains on and make it up the hill okay on my own. Lloyd got in his car, we all pushed as before, and he made it up the hill.

Then Lloyd, James, and Janet went ahead. I went back over to my car to put the chains on. As I took the chains out of the bag, I thought they sure don't look like they will fit on that tire. I checked the bag. They were 13" tire chains. I tried it over the tire but no way would it fit, so I threw them all back in the car. The truck driver was watching me. Then he offered to give you a push if I wanted to try it. No, I did not want to end up at the bottom of the canyon.

"Well, what are you going to do?" he asked.

"I guess just wait and maybe someone will show up. What are you going to do?"

He answered, "I have food and something to drink in my truck. I am going to stay here until the snow melts."

"Well, I guess I will stay here until someone comes by to help or also until the snow melts," I said.

With that, he pointed out, "I have been here since noon, it is almost five o'clock, and you are the only three cars I have seen all day." The truck driver asked, "Where do you live?"

When I told him I lived down in Seville he said, "You are a long way from home aren't you?"

I wondered how I got myself into this situation and hoped that maybe God would send someone else by to help me. We discussed what I was doing and what he was doing, just to pass the time. After about an hour, I heard an automobile coming up the mountain. I sure was excited when I heard his car coming up the mountain. I thought to myself, help is on the way. Sure enough, it was a Jaguar sedan with an English man, his wife, and two children. He stopped and asked what the problem was. I explained I needed a push up the hill and someone to keep it from sliding down into the canyon. It was rather amazing a carload of people and they all spoke English. We visited awhile. Then with them all pushing and holding it from sliding over the side, I drove right up the hill without a problem. I offered to come back to help them get through the dangerous part but he said that with all of his family and the truck driver he could get up the hill. I thanked them all very much and got in the car. I waved good-bye to them as I drove up the mountain. The roads were covered with heavy snow, with ruts and chuckholes in the packed snow, so I had to drive slow and very carefully.

I did find the other two cars at Mugaire, the intersection of the route that leads into Pamplona. They were waiting there for me wondering what had happened. I explained about the chains not fitting and having to wait for someone else to come along. I sure was glad to find them here. Now we needed to make tracks for Pamplona and hopefully find something to eat. Everyone was 100% ready for something to eat.

Lloyd took the lead again, and we drove reasonably slow considering the snow and bad roads. It was about 30 miles from Mugaire to Pamplona. It took a little over an hour to get there, but we found a very nice restaurant on the main street. Pamplona is the town where they have the annual running of the bulls and we were on the street they run down. But right now, we are more interested in a good square meal with something to drink.

We had a very good meal and plenty to eat. We had a bottle of wine among us and some gaseosa, as we were not only hungry, but also dry. After we finished dinner, James and Janet decided to get a hotel room and stay the night. Lloyd and I decided we would soldier on toward Zaragoza. We said our goodbyes to James and Janet. Lloyd took the lead. I told him that if I got so tired that I couldn't stay awake I would flash my lights a few times just in case he was about to go to sleep. We drove about two hours and I just could not stay awake any longer, so I flashed my lights three or four times. Lloyd flashed his brake lights and pulled off the first place that had enough room. When we stopped, I went up to Lloyd's car and asked him if he would like to sleep in my car since it had more room. We could leave the engine and heater running to keep us warm. Lloyd said that sounded like a very good idea. We both got in the front seat where it was warm and I think we were asleep before we sat down.

I slept a little over and hour. When I roused up a little, I noticed the heater didn't seem to be running as fast as it was when we first stopped. So I just turned the key off. This stopped the engine and heater and I went right back to sleep. Less than an hour later, I roused up again, and boy was it getting cold in the car. I wanted to be quiet, not to wake Lloyd up, so I just sat there and tried not to think about how cold it was. Before long, Lloyd woke up. He said he was cold and he couldn't even hear the engine running. I told him that when I woke up about 30 or 40 minutes ago, the heater wasn't running very good, so I turned the engine off.

I tried to start it again. It just went "Unk, unk" a couple of times, but then it started. I was sure surprised at that. Lloyd wanted to turn the heater on and try sleeping some more, but I didn't think that with the engine idling, it would keep the battery charged enough. I am so cold I didn't think I could go back to sleep, so I suggested we should just head for Madrid. I thought I would drive without the lights but if I saw a car coming, which wasn't likely, I would turn the lights on. I would turn the heater on after we had driven for a while to charge the battery. Lloyd said we should stop in Zaragoza to get gas. That sounded good to me, so we were on our way again.

We got to Zaragoza about ten o'clock a.m. We filled the cars with gas and got a cup of coffee to warm us up and help us to stay awake. I told Lloyd I had looked in the paperwork we got at customs and I found the address for the Fiat garage in Madrid. I was going directly there.

Lloyd lived on the base, which was before Madrid so he wished me luck with my car and hoped I would have a good trip to Seville. I had enjoyed sharing our experiences together the two days and nights and wished good luck to him also. I followed him to Torrejon Air Force Base, just in case my battery quit completely.

I made it all the way to the Fiat garage in Madrid at about four o'clock p.m. As I pulled up in front of the garage there was bar across the driveway with a guard in the guard shack. When he saw I was driving a Fiat he raised the bar and motioned me in.

I said, "La batería no function bien."

He pointed at a red door and said the mechanic was straight ahead. I drove over and went inside. I told the gentleman at the desk that I had a new Fiat, but the battery was dead. He told me the car would be ready in the morning at eight o'clock a.m. I thanked him and asked if there was a good hotel nearby. He said a driver would return in a couple of minutes and take me to the hotel. He was there almost immediately and took me to the hotel, which was a very short distance. I thanked him and went to check into the hotel. I went up to the room, took a shower, shaved, got dressed, and came back down to the restaurant. I was hungry and sleepy for I had not been to bed for three nights and really had only one good meal.

The waiter and I had quite a time with the menu. I understood very little Spanish and the waiter understood no English. So finally, he pointed to an item on the menu and said, "Es bueno." Then he tried to explain something else, of which I understood very little.

I said, "Es parecido pescado?"

He responded, "Si, señor."

So I motioned for him to bring it on. He eventually came out with a dish that had several white tubes about three quarters of an inch long and a half inch in diameter in some kind of sauce. I tried to eat it but it was like chewing on neoprene tubes and very tough. I couldn't eat it so I motioned for the waiter to come over. I shook my head indicating that I couldn't eat it.

I said, "Pescado por favor el gaseosa," and motioned with my hands to take this and bring me the fish.

It was not long until he was back with the fish and gaseosa to drink. I said, "Muchas gracias, the fish is very good." I ate the whole thing, drank all of the gaseosa, and left the waiter a good tip for putting up with this non Spanish-speaking customer. Now I was ready for a good night's sleep.

The next morning I was up about seven o'clock a.m. I got showered, got dressed, and went down for breakfast. I had a very good breakfast of Huevos Ranchero. There wasn't a long discussion with the waiter this time.

I went up to my room, got my suitcase, and walked a short distance to the garage. It was rather cold, but the sun was bright, which made it a nice brisk walk. It made me feel good. I was thinking today is going to be a good day. I went into the garage waiting room and gave the cashier the ticket for my car. He said my car would be right up. When I asked him if I owed anything, he said no, the car was fixed, no charge. When a nice shiny car drove up by the waiting room, I wondered if it was my car.

The man said, "Yes, we washed, waxed and cleaned out the inside. The problem with the car was the fan belt was loose. We fixed it, charged the battery, checked the alternator, everything is okay."

I got in it started right up. He opened the big garage door and I was on my way. I had already plotted my way out of town on the map. It wasn't long until I was out in the countryside with trees, open fields, no snow, and bright sunshine. Now I felt like I was finally on my way home. It felt good just cruising along in my new car with no traffic. This was the life! It was now early afternoon and I had just gone through Córdoba, the largest city between Madrid and Seville. I was almost home. Only about eighty miles yet to go.

All of a sudden, there were a bunch of 55-gallon drums filled with gravel setting right in the middle of the road. There were no signs, no warning of any kind. I saw tracks where other cars had pulled off to the right, so I did the same. I realized they were doing some repairs on the road. After about a quarter mile, I was pulling back onto the road where barrels were across the road here also. About that time, a Mercedes sedan came flying over the top of the hill doing about 100 miles an hour. He slammed on the brakes, locked up all of the wheels, and that thing was skidding as if it was on ice, headed right for me! I turned the wheels sharp to the right, headed back into the ditch I had just come out of to keep him from hitting me head on. He hit the left rear side, and ripped it up. I was furious! My new car wrecked before I got home! I jumped out of my car and started reading him the riot act in the few words of Spanish that I knew.

He kept saying, "Es nada, es nada."

I was trying to tell him what I thought in Spanish, but he kept saying "Es nada, es nada."

He was only making me more furious, so I ripped into him in English, "Es nada, my rear end! You wrecked my new car, before I even got home with it!" After letting off a little steam in English, my blood pressure went down and I asked him for his driver's license.

He understood nothing I said, so I took out my driver's license and showed him. He finally got the message and showed me his. I copied down his name, address, car license number, and other information I thought I needed and got back in my wrecked car and headed home. Not as happy as I was when I left Madrid, though.

When I got home, I started telling Peggy and the kids about all of my problems and the wrecked car.

Peggy said, "Wait until you hear what happened here while you were gone!" That will be another story.

BUYING AN MGB IN LONDON

It was February 1966. I was working at S.E.R.I.M.A. in Chateauroux, France. This company overhauled F-104 aircraft for the United States Strategic Air Command. A good friend of mine, Henri Renot, was an interpreter for this company. We both belonged to this French car club, Ecurie Berrichonne. Henri came over and asked me if I would like to go over to Ponitiers on Thursday night, about midnight to watch the Monte Carlo Rally cars from London. This was their first checkpoint after leaving London and headed over a specific route to Monte Carlo.

My answer, "You know I would like to go."

Since I was sure that my son, Dale Jr., would like to go too, I offered to drive. He asked me to come by about nine o'clock to pick him up. It is about 130 kilometers to Poitiers.

"You had better dress warm because between midnight and two o'clock a.m. it would be mighty cold," he warned.

That didn't bother me because I was all excited about seeing all of those rally cars. Sure enough, Dale Jr. wanted to go.

Peggy and Dale, Chateauroux, France, 1965.

Come Thursday night, Dale and I drove over to Henri's house. I knocked on the door and Henri came to the door. He was as excited as Dale and I were. He had a list of all of the cars entered in the rally. After looking over the list, I especially wanted to see John Sprinzel because he was entered in an MG. I wanted to buy a new MGB or Alfa Romeo Roadster before I went back to the U.S. in 1967. There was also a Ferrari V-12, Cooper S and other exotic cars entered. Henri knew some of the drivers and all about the cars because he had been a rally driver and a navigator also. As we piled in my Fiat 1800 4-door sedan and headed out, Henri said we might find some snow or ice on the road. We were still discussing the cars and drivers entered in the rally. We got there well before midnight but it wasn't long until the cars started coming into the checkpoint. The checkpoint was a large parking lot with a restaurant. The restaurant served hot drinks, including flaming grogs to keep your hands warm.

It wasn't long until John Sprinzel came in in the MG. So I went over and talked to him for a while. I told him I was interested in buying an American MGB Special. He told me to come by and see him at 33 Lancaster News there in London. I told him that I just might do that.

Soon the V-12 Ferrari came in and blipped the throttle three or four times. That got everyone's attention. I followed the crowd to check out the

V-12.

"Well, I would settle for one of these," I thought, "but my bank account said I had better settle for the MGB."

We all had a flaming grog before we left to warm up a bit because it was cold out there by one or two o'clock in the morning. But we sure were enjoying it. However, I will say it sure felt good to get into the car, especially when the heater came on good and hot.

As things progressed in 1966, Charles De Gaulé and the United States agreed to disagree. So the U. S. removed all of the military and all the government contracts out of France. I was disappointed about this because I was renting one-half of Chateau Brassioux, which had a nice green lawn, shrubbery, and many shade trees, and I had several friends in Ecurie Benishone. We spent quite a lot of time together, especially the holidays.

Dale in France, just bought some French bread. Holding a book, *Say it in French*. 1963.

In February of 1967, I was transferred to the procurement office in London, England. We rented a house at 50 The Avenue, in Watford, the western part of London. I was working out of the procurement office in London, traveling to many contracts throughout England, Oslo, Norway, the Island of Majorca, and one trip back to Chateauroux.

However, every now and then I thought about that John Sprinzel invitation to visit him at 33 Lancaster News. So in August of 1968, I got my maps of London and the underground routes, and decided what underground lines (the rapid transit system in London) I had to take to get there. Then one sunny afternoon I went out to see if John Sprinzel was there. He was.

One thing I remember he said was that he always told his partner that driving in the rallies helped sell cars. He was right because I bought the MGB there. A British racing green roadster. He turned me over to the salesman to see what cars they had available. He found the description of the one that I liked. So he said it is 130 pounds. But I was looking for a 10% discount.

"Why should I give you a discount?" he wanted to know.

My reply was, "You shouldn't give me a discount, but I will go somewhere else to buy it."

Dale in front of his house in CA with his two Ford Taurus SHOs and green MGB.

That British racing green MGB is sitting in my garage here in Simi Valley today, and I got the 10% discount. It came out to just under $1,500 American dollars.

SPORTS CAR OLYMPICS

I was at the Sports car Olympics, at Squaw Valley, California, in September 1969. I was with my son-in-law, Bob Daves. We were driving his 1962 Model 356 Porsche coupe. We changed the tires and wheels from the high performance street tires to racing slicks getting ready for the first autocross.

Now I have never driven any kind of Porsche in my life, so I asked Bob if I could drive his car down the street a little ways to see how it drives. He got in with me and I drove down the street a short distance making a few zigzags back and forth on the street to see how it handled. I tried the brakes a couple of times, accelerated pretty hard, up shifted and down shifted a couple of times.

I said, "I have this thing figured out. I am ready for my first run on the autocross course."

When we drove back, he said I could drive the car first in the race. We parked the car back in the pit area, and as we got out of the car, I said, "This is your car so you should drive first."

His reply was, "No you drive first."

After a little discussion back and forth he said, "Okay, I will drive first," which he did.

After the autocross was finished, we went over and checked our times. Bob was second and I placed fourth. Not too bad for our first autocross, but we would have to do better the next day.

Bob said, "Yeah I'm going to be in first place tomorrow."

I never said anything, but under my breath I was thinking, "Not if I can help it you won't."

The next day, we were out in the pit area changing tires and wheels back to the racing slicks again. We had driven a road rally the night before using the street tires. One of the competitors watching us changing tires came over and asked if we changed tires for every event. I told him if you want to win, you have to have the right equipment. He thought that was too much trouble and wouldn't go to all of that work.

When Bob and I finished putting on the racing tires he insisted that I drive first. I agreed since he seemed have his mind made up. I went over and got the car in lineup for the autocross. As I was sitting in the car waiting, I was thinking how exciting this is to drive fast through all of those curves and what fun it is. Now I'm thinking I am going to win this race. Every nerve, every muscle, and every thought has to know I am going to win. To down shift, brake, and up shift at the precise time. I have to know in my subconscious, that this is a rear engine car, and if it starts to plow off course I immediately have to lift off the throttle, so the weight will shift to the front wheels so the tires can bite into the asphalt and the car will go in the direction I steer it.

Every nerve, every muscle, and every thought has to know I am going to win.

It is my turn to go next. I blipped the throttle a couple of times to hear that roar and burbling of power. I needed to take off quickly, but not too much wheel spin, because I'll lose traction. Just the right amount of throttle, squeeze it on briskly. I got a good start, everything is going the way I planned until the last left hand turn to cross the finish line. It started to plow off course, headed right for the timing lights. I immediately lifted off the throttle. The front tires bit into the asphalt and headed for the finish line. I immediately nailed the throttle again and shot across the finish line. When they announced my time it was 35.15 hundredths of a second. That was fastest time so far, but there were several more cars to compete. Some were 911 six-cylinder Porsches. I noticed Bob looked worried. His smile had turned to a frown. He did not have much to say.

It finally came Bobs turn to drive. He gave it all he had. They announced his time of 35.17 seconds. I had first place by a mere two hundredths of a second. I finished first overall and Bob second. He was not too happy. Some of the other contestants told me I might have to take the greyhound bus home, because they did not think Bob was too happy about the results.

Dale's first racecar, 1972.

OVERHAULING A JAGUAR ENGINE

Rich Lach, a good friend of mine raced sports cars and motorcycles. He was in the hospital with a bad kneecap injury. He called me from the hospital one day and asked if I would be interested in overhauling the engine on a XK140 Jaguar for Dr. Ford, a friend of his there at the hospital.

"Yeah, I could do that. You know I am busy all the time, but eventually I could work it into my schedule," was my reply.

The next day, Dr. Ford called me and said he was told that I might be interested in overhauling his Jaguar's engine. I told him I was always very busy, but I would call him back within the next 10 days and let him know when to bring it over. He was all excited about the possibility of getting his Jag running again. In about a week, I called him at the hospital and told him to bring the Jag over that evening or the first thing the next day. He planned to come right after work. Sure enough, he was here a little after six o'clock and I had the garage ready.

Dr. Ford was all smiles as he got out of the car, "I sure will be glad to get this thing running again. And I have a few other things I want fixed also."

I said okay, but wanted to do the engine first. He wanted it overhauled sure, but anything that wasn't right he wanted it fixed too. I told him that is what I always do, I fix everything that is not correct, and it will run like a top. I gave him a ride back home in the Jag because I wanted to see how it ran. He lived in the housing tract just across Cochran Street from me. I told him I would call if I need anything or had any questions. That sounded good to him and he waved goodbye as I pulled out of the driveway in his Jaguar.

When I got home, I drove it right into the garage and started working on it. I removed the carburetors and noticed the fuel in the carburetors had a sour smell to it, which is a sign that it is very old and stale. That's not good for the engine. I removed all of the accessories, the intake and exhaust manifolds, and drained the engine oil, getting it ready to remove the engine the next day. The next morning I loosened all the cylinder head nuts, installed the engine hoist to the front and back cylinder head studs, so the engine was evenly balanced and easily removed, and hooked up the hoist to the cable drive winch. With the front of the Jaguar jacked up and on jack stands, I tightened up the winch just enough to put a little pressure on it, then removed the bolts that attach the transmission to the engine.

Then I put more weight on the hoist and removed the nuts and bolts that attach the engine to the mounts. Now I was ready to crank the cable hoist and pull the engine up and out of the car. I removed the oil pan and the cylinder head, keeping all the nuts and bolts separated into separate containers according to what part they were removed from. I removed all of the rod bearings, caps, rods and pistons, making sure all caps were replaced on the rods they were removed from. Next, I took off the timing cover, timing gears, camshaft bearing caps and camshaft, also be sure all bearing caps are replaced in the exact place they were removed from.

When I removed the engine, I noticed the starter gear had chewed all the flywheel ring gear teeth. I ordered a new ring gear right away because I had to measure the inside diameter of the ring gear in four different places, to get the average inside dimension. I needed that to get the flywheel machined to the proper dimension, which is two and a half thousands larger than the ring gear. When you heat the ring-gear red to white hot, and install it on the flywheel, it cools down and will be as solid as one piece of metal. In fact, as solid as the Rock of Gibraltar.

I placed the engine on the floor, removed all of the main bearing caps, and marked them with a 3-cornered file, the marks related to the position of each bearing cap. Then I removed the crankshaft and measured all of the rod and main journals. They were all within the dimensions of a new crankshaft.

With help, I loaded the engine block and the cylinder head in the van and took them down to Big T's machine shop there in Simi Valley. I told big T I wanted a complete valve job on the cylinder head and hot tank the block. If it needed more than ridge reaming and honing the cylinder walls, I needed to know right away, so I could order the parts. Big T said he would call before noon the next day to let me know if I needed to order any special parts. I had plenty to keep me busy. I had ordered a new ring gear for the flywheel, but I needed to get the flywheel machined to fit the ring gear. These Jaguars were not like most cars. Big T wished me luck, which I would need working on that Jaguar.

When I got home, I got a tablet and wrote down a list of parts I needed to overhaul the engine. Then I got to thinking, I don't really like to clean all of these parts, so I guess I better get at it. The oil pan, valve cover, intake and exhaust manifolds, timing gear cover, timing gears and chain and the carburetors all had to be cleaned. I smelled that sour gasoline again, so I called Dr. Ford and asked him how often he drove the Jag. The gas smelled sour so I wanted to know if it ran okay. He had only had it a few months, but he drove it occasionally, and it seemed to run okay. So I finished cleaning the parts and put them on the other workbench.

The next morning after I finished mowing the lawn, the UPS driver showed up with my flywheel ring gear. I took it out to the back garage and laid it on top of the flywheel to see if the outside of the ring gear would line up with the flywheel teeth. It seemed to be the right diameter to engage with the starter gear. I took the four measurements, 90 degrees apart, of the inside diameter of the ring gear, wrote down the numbers meticulously to the nearest ten thousandths. Then I added the four numbers together and divided that sum by 4 and added 25 thousandths to that sum. I needed the flywheel machined to that dimension. I took the flywheel and ring gear to a machine shop in Canoga Park that I always used.

I showed Don, the owner, the flywheel and he said, "I think you should take that flywheel to see the dentist. It doesn't have any teeth left."

I showed him the new ring gear and asked him to machine the flywheel to 25 thousandths larger than the ring gear. I gave him the measurements I had and he said he would double-check all of the measurements. We didn't want to machine it too small, and then I would need to buy a new flywheel. I told him to give me a call when he had it finished. He said it might take a couple of days as he had quite a backlog. But he always did excellent work, so I was sure this would be also.

When I returned home, I called Terry at Big T's. He had the block ready. He told me he had used the ridge reamer to cut that ridge out of the top of the cylinder and power honed all of the cylinders, to break the glaze.

They all cleaned up real good at standard bore dimensions. I was glad to hear that. Now I could order all of the parts to overhaul the engine. I told Terry I would see him the next day and pick up everything then.

ATLANTA AIRPORT, WHEN THINGS START GOING WRONG

"What do you mean you don't have a pilot and crew for the flight to Evansville? It is supposed to depart in five minutes," the agent stated. "I know but the pilot and crew have not arrived."

But in two or three minutes, we started loading the plane. As I am standing in line getting my driver's license and boarding pass ready for the loading security check, I see that I have seat 8A. I thought to myself, "That is great. I have a seat up front next to the window." They checked my driver's license and boarding pass and asked if anyone had given me anything to take aboard the airplane or if I have any sharp instruments. I told them no.

As I walked through the doorway, I see the other passengers getting in this small twin prop jet engine airplane. I am about the last passenger loaded, and seat 8A is next to the back seat of the airplane. It is also the window and aisle seat since there is only one row of seats on this side.

About the time, I got to my seat the pilot announced, "We have been waiting here for 30 to 40 minutes for the passengers." I once heard this saying that cheap labor is false economy. We were waiting 30 minutes to load and the pilot and crew are in the airplane waiting for passengers.

Then the pilot announced, "Air Force One just landed with President George W. Bush aboard, and no planes could move or land anywhere on the airport until the president is out of the airport area."

At least President Bush was not like ex-president Clinton, who had his barber come aboard Air Force One to give him a haircut, keeping the entire airport shut down for about an hour while he got a haircut.

After about twenty minutes the pilot announced, "The airport is clear for us to depart."

But we were still sitting there. In a few minutes, the pilot came back on to say, "The engine wouldn't start. We will call a mechanic to fix it.

I thought to myself, I should ask for a refund and rent a car to drive the 750 miles to Evansville, because I don't trust this airplane. Now we are waiting another twenty minutes or so for the mechanic.

After a while, he did get the engine started, but then the pilot reported, "I'm not getting the right readings on the engine instruments, so we will have to get a different airplane."

I was glad to hear that. They had all passengers unload and go to concourse C26 and wait for further instructions. Another ten to fifteen minutes of waiting and we were sent to Concourse 31 to board a different airplane. We proceeded to Concourse 31 and waited another fifteen minutes for that airplane. We all had to go through the security check again with picture ID and boarding pass. Finally, everyone got on and the plane was ready to go.

After a while, the pilot announced that five passengers would have to get off because this airplane had a different configuration than the other one, and we were way over our maximum load. So we still weren't going anywhere. After another long wait, the Majordomo came aboard the airplane, saying five passengers would have to get off the airplane. Delta was offering $300, one thousand frequent flier miles, dinner that night, and a later flight to Evansville to anyone that would volunteer. Two people volunteered, so that meant three of us would be kicked off.

He continued, "We are still overloaded. If you are a frequent flyer, you have first priority. We only have seven passengers that are not frequent flyers, and three of you will have to get off."

I had a very slim chance of surviving this. The Majordomo got the list of passengers and started calling off names. My name was the last one called. The other two passengers got off.

He had the list and seat number assignments, so he came back to me and said, "Are you Dale Ragel?"

I said, "Yes, and if I have to get off I guess I will, but my brother-in-law, nephew, and his wife are at the airport in Evansville waiting for me now. I have to be there to go to my sister's funeral tomorrow."

He studied the list again and said he would call the next person on the list, which he did. That individual got up, got his carry-on baggage, and left the plane. Now we are finally ready to depart. But no, the Majordomo now announces that we have to wait until the baggage handlers come out and go through all of the luggage to find and remove the bags that belong to the five people that got off the airplane. I thought to myself with luck we might get out of here before midnight. This whole thing reminded me of what an old airline pilot told me back in September of 1962.

He said, "If you have time to spare, go by air."

REPLACING PALMDALE APARTMENT STAIRS

It was June 9, 2002. Terry, a contractor friend from church, and I went to Palmdale to check out the stairs that go up to the second floor of the apartment building that I own there.

The manager, Anita Johnson, had called me a couple of times, telling me that the stairs needed repair. After a close look at them, I realized they didn't need to be repaired. Everything needed to be replaced. The stairs, the railing, the second story deck, and railing all needed to be entirely replaced. Neither Terry nor I had time to work on it right away.

We went to Home Depot to get some steel braces to attach the stairs to the upper deck's two by twelve faceplates, and to brace the upper stairs to the midway-landing platform.

We couldn't start work immediately because Terry had two jobs he was working on, and Ann and I had a reservation in Palm Springs. We were going for a one-week stay to celebrate our seventh wedding anniversary. We would only be home about ten days before leaving July second for our six-week summer vacation. That is another story.

On November 19, we finally got started on the stairs and deck replacement. We went to Home Depot in Palmdale. Terry walked up to the Pro Desk and asked if an order for a load of lumber and building material made today could be delivered today.

"No, we take the order one day and deliver it the next day," was their reply.

Terry asked if where there was a Terry Lumber yard in Palmdale. They answered that there was one about a mile east on Avenue P, just over the railroad track. As the clerk said, "Avenue P," Terry was on his way out the door.

When we arrived at Terry Lumber, we went immediately to the order desk. Terry asked, "If we order a load of lumber now, can you deliver it today?"

"I will find out," he replied as he picked up the phone. After a short pause he said, "We can deliver it right after lunch."

I gave him the list of material we needed, then Terry and I picked out the nuts, bolts, lag bolts, screws, and glue that we needed. When I paid for the hardware the clerk said, "Your lumber will be there by one-thirty."

I said, "I sure hope so because we are going to tear down all of the stairs right now."

Terry brought a helper, Julio, along to help. Julio was already at work tearing down the stairs when we got back to the apartment. Now, all three of us ripped into the stairs, tearing it apart. We stacked the heavy lumber on the lawn by the stairs, the two by fours and lighter pieces; we stacked just over the fence by the carport, and put the smaller pieces in the dumpster.

About two o'clock, Terry's cell phone rang. It was Terry Lumber Company. Their truck driver was in a wreck with the truck and he was in the hospital. So they wouldn't be able to deliver the lumber until tomorrow. I felt sorry for the driver, but I thought to myself we are in trouble now.

Terry said, "Look! We have some people up stairs that can't get down. And some will be coming home from work in a few hours and they can't get upstairs. I need that lumber today! As soon as you can possibly get it here!" They said they would have it here today, as soon as possible. We tried to rent portable stairs but nobody rents them anymore because they can't afford the liability insurance.

We finished tearing the stairs down, cleaned up the area, and got everything ready to start building the stairs as soon as the lumber truck got there. The truck arrived about four-thirty.

I told the driver, "Unload it right here in the corner."

As he got out of the truck he said, "We had to change the order on some of the lumber so I need..."

"Yes I know, I have a check right here for $61.92. They called me on the phone and explained it to me, but we urgently needed the lumber now."

He took the check, gave me the receipt, and then he tilted the bed up on the truck until the ends of the lumber touched the ground. Then he drove the truck out from under the load of lumber. When that $1,600 worth of lumber hit the driveway, it sounded like a bomb exploded.

I said, "Let's carry the 4 x 4's, 2 x 12's, and 2 x 6's back there by the saw, so we can get started building that landing first."

We all started carrying lumber back to the saw, until we had enough to build the first landing and a set of stairs for each of the two sides of the landing. Terry and Julio started measuring and cutting the corner posts and the 2 x 12's for the step runners. I set up the two tripods of lights as it was beginning to get dark by now. I set one of the lights to shine on the saw table and the other to shine where we were building the first landing.

Terry asked me to drill the holes in the corner posts and get a couple of wrenches to tighten the bolts. The corner posts were to be bolted to the four metal brackets that were already in the cement from the stairs that we had just demolished.

"Okay, Terry! I will hold the corner post upright here, if you will adjust it to exactly where you want it and mark where you want the holes drilled," I said.

As we marked the holes on the last post Terry said, "Be sure you drill the holes straight through so the bolt will align with the bracket hole on the opposite side."

I could do that, even if I needed to drill it from both sides. Terry measured and marked the six step runners. There were three for each side; one set of steps for the carport side and steps on the opposite side for the visitor's parking lot. Julio was sawing the step runners and Terry helped me align all of the bolt holes to the brackets.

I got the bolts and drove them through the post and brackets, installing the washers and nuts just snug, not tight. He cut the 2 x 12's that we will bolt on all four sides, at the top of these 4 x 4 posts. The 2 x 12's will support the midway deck and all nine of the step runners from the ground up to the midway deck on both sides and from the midway deck to the second floor deck.

When Terry brought the four 2 x 12's over we started drilling holes again. We drilled two holes in each end of the 2 x 12's and four holes in the top end of the 4 x 4 posts; that was a total of twenty-four three-quarter inch holes in the 4 x 4's and a total of sixteen holes in the 2 x 12's. After we installed the sixteen bolts in the top of the 4 x 4's and attached the 2 x 12's we tightened the bolts just snug and checked that everything was square and level. Then we started tightening all of the bolts tight, checking often to be sure that everything was square and level.

When that was finished, Terry announced, "I sure could use a cup of hot coffee."

By now, it was almost ten o'clock p.m. and we had not eaten anything since lunch. So I offered to go to McDonalds and get some coffee and cold drinks. Terry and Julio started attaching the step runners to the 2 x 12's on the mid-deck with metal brackets made specifically for that purpose. When I got back with the drinks, we took about a three-minute break and went right back to work. We all worked diligently because we wanted to go home before daylight the next day. Terry and Julio finished hanging the step stringers and I started attaching the steps, Julio had already cut. They were redwood 2 x 6's, four feet long. We used two boards for each step. They were attached to the stringers with six deck screws in each 2 x 6 board. We finally got all of the steps installed on one side up to the deck, and then we installed 2 x 6 planks on the mid-deck. They were six feet long and stuck out about two feet over the sidewalk.

I said, "We better cut these ends off or someone will run into them."

Terry replied, "I will bring in my circular saw tomorrow and cut them all off at once so they will all be exactly even on the other end."

"We need to get some kind of steps from this mid-deck to the upper deck so these people can go to work in the morning."

Terry said, "I know, I'm going to try to install the new steps, but we can't do that until we get the fascia board on the top deck, to attach the step stringers to. We will have to make something temporary."

We used the old step stringers, which were 4" x 10', and very heavy. We got them both in place, and then we attached the steps with angle iron brackets to the stringers. It was after midnight. We still had to put up temporary banisters to both sets of steps and put up red caution tape on the side where there are no steps. By the time all of that is finished it is after one o'clock in the morning. We still have to carry all of the lumber in from the front parking lot to the courtyard by the side of the building. Then drive the 65 miles home before we can go to bed.

The next day, Wednesday, the day for my writing class (a good excuse), I didn't go to work. Also, I didn't feel like getting up at five-thirty a.m. and driving to Palmdale.

Thursday I went back. They had the new fascia board on the upper deck and the new stairs attached to it. We went to work installing the 4 x 4 posts and the railing for the banisters. About eleven o'clock a.m. I was helping install the banisters. Now, when I work I am usually very diligent about it. I go charging around like a mad bull with my head down. I ran right into those mid-deck floor planks that stuck out over the sidewalk, "Oh!" I cried, "Terry I told you someone is going to run into those things."

"Are you hurt?" he asked.

"No, I'm okay," I said, as I picked up my cap and glasses I felt a little gash on the bridge of my nose.

Terry went to get a Band-Aid out of his truck.

"No! I'm okay," I insisted.

"Well, you need a Band-Aid on it so you can wear your glasses," he said.

"Okay. If you insist," I finally said.

After we fixed my nose, we went back to work on the stairs and banisters. Terry and I were measuring and cutting the 4 x 4 posts for the rest of the stairs and Julio was measuring, cutting, pre-drilling and installing the red wood spindles for the lower deck on the east side.

About twelve-thirty, I said, "If you guys are hungry we can go and get some dinner."

"We need some more deck screws, so we could stop by Home Town

Buffet for dinner and then pick up some deck screws from Home Depot," Terry replied.

It is a good thing we went to Home Town Buffet for dinner because Terry and Julio can sure put the food away. I was a little more conservative as I always want to leave a little room for ice cream and desert. I think we all enjoyed dinner. We stopped at Home Depot and got the deck screws.

On our way back to work Terry asked me, "Can you take Julio home this evening, because I have an appointment to deliver a bid on a job in Northridge, and I have to discuss it with the customer at three-thirty this afternoon?"

Repairing apartment roof at the age of 86. Undated photo.

"Sure, I can do that if Julio directs me to where he wants to go."

Julio chimed in, "Yeah! I have a car and I know my way around in the Valley. I can direct you to where my car is parked."

By this time, we were back working on the stairs with sawdust flying everywhere and drilling the 4 x 4 corner posts and railings trying to get the stairs completed enough that the tenants living on the second floor could get up and down the stairs.

About two-thirty p.m., someone walked up to where we were working and started a conversation with Terry. The conversation turned into a heated argument. Before they got into a fight, I went over to where they were and told him, "I am the owner of the building."

He introduced himself as the Palmdale building and safety officer, and said, "We got a call from a lady that said she had no way to get down stairs."

I explained, "That is why we are working so diligently here to get the steps completed."

He asked, "Do you have a building permit?"

"No!" I answered, "I never applied for a building permit because these stair stringers are all rotted out where they are attached to the upper deck. And the faceplate they are attached to is all rotten wood. Friends have told me, they applied for a building permit and sometimes it took five to six months to get an approval. I wanted this thing repaired now, so I started working on it."

He said, "Well you can't do any more work on it until you submit a drawing with the material you are using and a plan for the work to be accomplished and get a permit."

I said, "These stairs and deck don't look very safe to me without a hand rail, are you going to be responsible if someone gets hurt."

He answered, "No! I will give you until four p.m. to install temporary hand rails."

I said, "Just Julio and are I here now and we cannot install temporary hand rails by four p.m."

"Okay, here is my card, give me a call when you get it completed. How long do you think it will take?" he asked.

"I don't know, but probably three to four hours," I replied.

"Just give me a call and I will come out to take a look at it," he said.

So Julio and I went to work gathering up any 2 x 4's, 2 x 6's, or 2 x 12's that we could use for the banisters and supports for them. We had to use some new 2" x 6" x 12' redwood for the top handrail and we secured everything with deck screws, using screw guns to put everything together. When we finished I called the number he left us to let him know. Their office is less than a half of a mile from where we were working so he was there in just a couple of minutes. There were a couple of things he didn't like that we had to fix, but we were on our way home by about seven-thirty. This was about average, as I usually got home somewhere between seven and nine p.m.

We didn't get the drawings and plans ready until December 3. I took them to Palmdale and got the permit that day. But the first day back to work was December 13. So for 21 days we didn't work on the apartment.

Our first day back to work I went out to Terry's truck, which was parked in the carport area, to get an extension cord so we could plug in our battery charger for the cordless drills.

I was taking a short cut across the lawn when Terry hollered at me, "You just stepped in that pile of dog doo-doo."

He and Julio were laughing their heads off. I looked down at my shoe and that yellow stuff was squirting out on all sides of my shoe sole.

I said, "Oh sh__."

So I went and got a screwdriver and some paper towels to clean off my shoe sole at the water faucet in front of the apartment.

When I came back they were still laughing so I said, "Ok you both owe me $5 apiece for entertainment fees."

Of course, we all had a good laugh about that and went back to work. The next twenty workdays were about like the first two days before the building inspector shut us down. We finished on February 6, then on February 8, Ann and I drove to Phoenix, Arizona, for a 50th wedding anniversary, and from there on to Texas to visit our daughters and families for the next two weeks.

STRESS MEASURING MACHINE BLEW A FUSE

It was about six-thirty a.m. on December 8. We got a phone call from our sister-in law, Vera Hoffart that her son John Hoffart, a Simi Valley policeman, had been in a horrible accident in the police car while chasing the driver of a stolen car. John was unconscious on a ventilator in the intensive care unit at Simi Valley Hospital with head and internal injuries. We immediately prayed for John's healing from this accident and Ann called many of the family to inform them of the accident.

I was already stressed out about a letter I got from the City of Simi Valley on December 4 that the house I own on Angela Street in Simi Valley was in violation, because they had not paid for trash collection. If it were not paid in full by the 8th, I would be fined $100. And if it were not taken care of on the eighth, the fine would escalate to $200 for the second offense, and $500 for the third offense. I felt this was a pretty stiff fine for not paying to have trash pickup. This is supposed to be a free country, a government of the people, by the people, and for the people, not against the people.

My lease states the lessee is responsible to pay all utilities, so I called the tenant about this and said she had paid it with her credit card on the internet. I called the trash company. No! She had not paid for trash pickup. They didn't have a system where you can pay by credit card on the internet. Well, she told me she paid it that way. I was very skeptical, because I have trouble collecting the rent. I called the tenant back and told her if it was not settled by the end of the day I would start eviction papers on her, because she was also behind in paying the rent.

Now to add to this stress factor, on Mondays we have the three grandchildren, ages 4 to 13 years old, that have stayed the night. Ann gets Ryan, the 13-year-old, up in time to review all of his homework before he goes to school.

When Ann got home from taking Ryan to school, the 7 year old, Jenna, which Ann also home schools, got up complaining her fingers were stiff she could hardly move them, and she complained that she itched all over her body and her legs. Her legs, body, and face had large red whelps covering over half of her body. I didn't know, but it could be hives. Ann didn't know either, but called Jenna's Mother at work to see what she wanted to do. Theresa left work to come home and take her to the doctor. The next day, Jenna had an appointment with an allergist. She still breaks out with a rash.

About eight-thirty this same morning we get another phone call. This time from Texas. It is our son-in-law Jim Parker. He wanted to know if we could do him a favor. I asked him what he had in mind.

He said, "Well I called the bank this morning to see if I could pick up the money from the loan we had applied for on the twenty acres where we live. They informed me that the IRS has a $13,000 lean against our property." Jim knew nothing about lean. Jim said, "If you can help me out we can pay you back in about ten days."

I agreed and asked for his bank name and account number. I could transfer it from my account to his. I got all the info that I needed, got my checkbook, and was looking in the phone book for our bank telephone number. I could not find our bank in the phone book.

Pay attention to your wife, because she is usually right!

Ann, looking in another phone book, said, "The Bank of America telephone number is…"

"What are you giving me the Bank of America number for? I haven't had a bank account there for 30 years."

Right then is when the fuse blew on our stress meter!

I had found the phone number for our bank. I called them and they said they couldn't transfer the money to another bank, but for $15, they could wire it to them.

When I hung up the phone, Ann reminded me that a couple of years ago we went to the Bank of America there in Simi and deposited money into their account for them.

"I don't remember that," I said.

"Well we did," was her reply.

So after I cooled down a little, I took our checkbook, went down to Bank of America there in Simi, and deposited $13,000 in their account in Dallas, Texas. No problem.

The lesson learned in this experience is, pay attention to your wife, because she is usually right!

John Hoffart was still in intensive care in UCLA Hospital on the respirator. He seemed a little more alert the day before, but keeps his eyes closed most of the time, and has a slight case of pneumonia. John was in the hospital a long time with many injuries. He has recovered as well as can be expected and is lucky to be alive.

RUDE AWAKENING

After breakfast on Monday morning, September 6, 2004, my wife Ann and I went over to my house of 36 years on Marilyn Street in Simi Valley, to see what it looked like. The tenants had moved to Texas, while we were gone on a six-week vacation. They had given us a key to the front door before we left on our vacation. So with key in hand I walked up to the front door and instead of that big brass door handle and long brass engraved plate on the front door, there was the key end of a dead bolt, staring me in the face.

I turned to Ann and said, "What in the world is going on here, this is our house isn't it?"

As I looked down the street to be sure, "Well Shirley said none of the door keys would fit," was Ann's reply.

I tried all of the keys again, but with no luck. We rang the doorbell, and knocked on the door. No answer. We walked around the house and tried the sliding doors and all of the windows they were all locked. So we tried the doorbell and knocked on the front door again. No luck.

I said, "This sure is a bummer. My and I family lived here 28 years now I can't even get in my own home."

We came back two more times that day and evening hoping to find someone home. No luck. We went through the same thing Tuesday, but never got an answer.

Wednesday morning we went over and went through the same routine ringing the doorbell, knocking on the door, but no answer. So Ann and I walked out to our car in the driveway.

I said, "I think I will call the police, because we aren't making any progress here."

I told them what had been going on, that someone was in my house that was vacant, and I couldn't get in. I explained there was a dead bolt on the front door in place of a doorknob.

They said they would be right out, and just give them the address.

While waiting in the driveway for the police to come, our cell phone rang. Ann checked to see who was calling. It was our phone number from my house we were sitting in front of.

Ann gave me the phone. As I answered it a voice said, "This is J.P."

I said, "Well come and open the door, because I am standing right here in the driveway."

"I am at work. I am not in the house."

"Well the lights are on in the house and I am talking to you on my telephone number in this house."

"No I am at work. That is my girlfriend in the house."

"Well tell her to come and open the door."

"No she won't, but I'll be out by ten o'clock tomorrow night."

After a little argument over the phone I said, "I want you out now!"

Within a few minutes, two police cars came around the corner. They stopped about three to four houses just west of my house. As they walked up to us, I showed them the dead bolt in the front door. They tried all of the doors and windows again but they were all locked.

When we came back to the front door the policemen said, "We can break down the front door, if that is what you want."

"No I have a drill and a set of drill bits in the trunk. I will just drill the lock out."

As I was drilling away, we heard a thump noise. I stopped drilling for a minute, but we never heard anything else. I drilled a few more seconds and the lock just fell out.

I pushed the door open and started to go in, but the policeman said, "You wait here. We will go in and see if anyone is in there."

The two policemen went in with their guns drawn, so I waited until they came back. They said, "We looked in the attic and everywhere the place is empty, but there is a pan of hot water on the stove. The fire was turned off."

We thanked the police for coming out and that they helped us get back into my own house. Ann and I checked out the whole house. They had set up housekeeping as if this was their home; bed and television in the master bedroom; couch, TV, and wall unit in the living room; food and beer in the refrigerator; garage half-full of construction tools. It was just as if they planned on living there until someone showed up to claim their house.

We went back through the house deciding what all needed to be done to get it ready to rent. It needed a lot of cleaning, painting, and replacing several items.

The next day J.P. and his girlfriend came and took out two truckloads of furniture and put the rest of their belongings in the garage. Then we went about cleaning and painting of walls, ceiling and base boards.

Ann did a lot of cleaning in the kitchen and bathrooms.

One Saturday as we pulled up in front of the house to do more cleaning, there was a pickup truck there. They were loading the rest of their stuff from the garage. When I unlocked the front door and went in, I noticed the door from the family room to the garage was open, which we always kept locked. As we walked into the family room, we were walking in water.

I asked Ann, "Where in the world did all this water come from."

"I don't know" she replied, as she grabbed a couple of our cleaning towels and started wiping up the water in the kitchen and family room.

I helped for a while then I went out and asked J.P., "Where did all this water come from?"

"I don't know, but I will fix it," he said, not even looking up.

"When are you going to fix it?"

"I will go unload this and be back in about 30 minutes."

This was September 18 and I haven't seen him since.

Our dishwasher was on that truckload somewhere, but we didn't notice that until he was gone. We had the carpet stretched and cleaned. I installed a new control valve and solenoids in the refrigerator. And I installed a new dishwasher and ran a couple of cycles before we went home. Everything worked good.

On October 1, the new tenants moved in.

THE BEST MOTHER OF THE YEAR

My wife, Ann Ragel, is the best Mother of the year. Her 3 grandchildren call her Nana. They live here in Simi and are from 4 to 13 years old. And almost every week if we are home, one of them want to come and stay all night with us. Sometimes the two girls 4 & 6 both want to come together but mostly one at a time, because they want Nana's undivided love and attention. Jenna, the 6 year old, likes to stay on Tuesday night, because she wants to go to the Tuesday night bible study with us.

Also, when we read the bible in the mornings, Ryan the 13 year old, and Jenna take their turns in reading. Then I lead the prayers and we all pray. When we are over to their house or they are over here, Jenna gets up on Nana's lap and whispers in her ear, "Can I stay with you tonight," or, "Can I go home with you?"

On March 9, 2002, my daughter, Shirley, fell on the sidewalk in front of Mann Theater. She couldn't get up and they had to call the ambulance to take her to the hospital. Her right shoulder was broken right at the joint. Ann went over every morning to get Shirley's breakfast, and usually took her something for dinner. Ann also took Shirley to the doctor, shopping, or wherever she needed to go. Ann also fed the cat every day. She did this for three or four weeks until Shirley was able to do a few things for herself.

A few years ago, Ann's daughter Theresa had major surgery. So Theresa and her 3 children, 10 months to 9 years of age, stayed with us for about 3 weeks or so until Theresa got her strength back. Ann cooked for everyone, gave Theresa four shots a day, kept track of her medication, and took care of the children because Theresa's husband worked out of town at that time. I wasn't much help since I had hernia operation at about the same time. For a few days, Ann had to help me also. Ann has been a very good mother to all of our children, grandchildren, and great grandchildren. She likes to help people whenever she can.

Peggy and Dale, and our 14 grandchildren. Photo taken during Dale's 90th birthday party.

Peggy, my first wife, had started making an afghan that is made in strips, called a Mile-A-Minute afghan. But when she got sick, was unable to finish it. I never parted with it.

After Ann and I were married awhile I said, "Peggy started an afghan for our granddaughter Cynthia Vidaurreta. Do you think you could finish it or want to?"

"I think I can. Let me see what it looks like."

So I got the out box with the afghan and many skeins of yarn.

Ann looked at it and said, "I am sure I can finish it.

After finishing what she was working on, she started on this afghan. When it was finished, we took it to Texas, and one evening when the Vidaurreta's were all home, we took it over and Ann presented it to Cynthia.

As she was taking it out of the box with tears in her eyes, she said to Ann, "I can just feel the love that grandma and you put into making this afghan. It sure is a blessing to me."

As I am writing this, Ann is weaving a blue ribbon around the outer edge of the blanket she just finished for Cynthia's youngest son Aaron Paul, born April 27, 2003.

Ann has crocheted baby blankets and has made a baby blanket from this soft heavy baby blanket material with appropriate color silk binding sewed around the outer edge. She has done this for all of my great grandchildren born since we were married.

All of the great grandchildren are always very glad to see Grandma Ann when we go to Texas to visit them.

PHOTOGRAPHS

Wedding portrait of Myrtle Ann Stein Ragel and Joseph Russell Ragel, 1908.

Above: Virgil, Eugene, and Dale. Undated photo.

Left: Dale and two milk buckets, 1926.

Above: Ragel family portrait. Left to right: Virgil, Dale, Nola, Russ, Herbert, Eugene, and Vida. Undated photo.

Joseph Russell "Russ" Ragel. Undated photo.

Top: Wedding photo of Peggy and Dale Ragel. February 1926

Center: Peggy, Shirley, and Dale Ragel. Undated photo.

Bottom: Peggy, Dale, Shirley, Vicky, and Dale Jr., in San Lorenzo, 1954.

Left: Dale and his well at his home at 184 Via Esperanzo. June 1955.

Right: Ragel family. Easter Sunday, 1955.

Peggy and Dale, San Lorenzo, 1958.

Dale home on leave from working overseas. August 1955.
Top photo: Back row: Alice, Richard, June, Peggy, Shirley, Dale
Front row: Donna, Charles, Greg, Vickie, Dale Jr.
Below: Peggy and Dale

35th Anniversary Photo, Peggy and Dale, 1977.

Dale and Peggy's 50th Wedding Anniversary. 1992.

Dale's Racecar. Undated photo.

Ann and Dale. Undated photo.

Dale's 90th Birthday.

Uncle Carl Roser and Dale Ragel. July 2002.

Dale Edwin Ragel, Sr, 2011

FAMILY TREE

FATHER

Joseph Russell Ragel

Birth: Aug 22 1880 in St. James, Illinois

Death: Dec 09 1955 in St. James, Illinois

Marriage: Feb 27 1908

Father: Josephus Ragel

Mother: Josephine Milnor

Other Spouses: Edna

Other Spouses: Juanita

MOTHER

Myrtle Ann Stine

Birth: Jan 13 1887 in Fayette, Illinois

Death: Feb 27 1922 in Carmargo, Illinois

Father: William Monroe Stine

Mother: Nancy Matilda Lowry

CHILDREN

Nola Ruth Ragel

Birth: Feb 24 1909 in Loogootee, Illinois

Death: Nov 20 2001 in Marietta, Georgia

Marriage: Feb 24 1933 in Champaign, Illinois

Spouse: Harold Elisha Fulfer

Vida Lucy Ragel

Birth: Oct 09 1911 in St. James, Illinois

Death: Nov 2001

Marriage: Dec 25 1932 in Enfield, Illinois

Spouse: Carl A. Roser

Herbert Russell Ragel

Birth: 1913 Oct in St. James, Illinois

Marriage: Oct 21 1945

Spouse: Elsie Manning

Virgil Williams Ragel

Birth: Mar 02 1916 in St. James, Illinois

Death: 1955 in Champaign, Illinois

Marriage: 1944 in Champaign, Illinois

Spouse: Elna Shroeder

Eugene Robert Ragel

Birth: Nov 25 1918 in St. James, Illinois

Death: Nov 22 1982 in Arizona

Marriage: Aug 01 1953 in Lordsbury, New Mexico

Spouse: Dorothy Perri

Dale Edwin Ragel

Birth: Aug 20 1920 in St. James, Illinois

Death: Nov 1 2012 in California

Marriage: May 09 1942 in Missouri

Spouse: Peggy J. Pulliam

Other Spouses: Ann Hoffert

Made in the USA
Middletown, DE
02 April 2023

28120807R00137